THE PASSENGER

BEFORE YOU START TO READ THIS BOOK, take this moment to think about making a donation to punctum books, an independent non-profit press,
@ https://punctumbooks.com/support/
If you're reading the e-book, you can click on the image below to go directly to our donations site. Any amount, no matter the size, is appreciated and will help us to keep our ship of fools afloat. Contributions from dedicated readers will also help us to keep our commons open and to cultivate new work that can't find a welcoming port elsewhere. Our adventure is not possible without your support.
Vive la open-access.

*Fig.* 1. Hieronymus Bosch, *Ship of Fools* (1490–1500)

THE PASSENGER: MEDIEVAL TEXTS AND TRANSITS Copyright © 2017 by the editor and authors. This work carries a Creative Commons BY-NC-SA 4.0 International license, which means that you are free to copy and redistribute the material in any medium or format, and you may also remix, transform and build upon the material, as long as you clearly attribute the work to the authors (but not in a way that suggests the authors or punctum books endorses you and your work), you do not use this work for commercial gain in any form whatsoever, and that for any remixing and transformation, you distribute your rebuild under the same license. http://creativecommons.org/licenses/by-nc-sa/4.0/

First published in 2017 by punctum books, Earth, Milky Way.
https://punctumbooks.com
ISBN-13: 978-1-947447-36-3 (Print)
ISBN-13: 978-1-947447-37-0 (ePDF)
LCCN: 2017960536
Library of Congress Cataloging Data is available from the Library of Congress

Copy editing: Matt Ossias
Interior design: Vincent W.J. van Gerven Oei
Cover design: Chris Piuma
Cover image: Orange County Airport, c. 1967. Photo courtesy Orange County Archives.

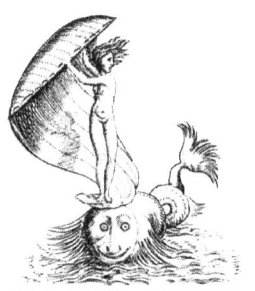

HIC SVNT MONSTRA

# THE PASSENGER
MEDIEVAL TEXTS AND TRANSITS
JAMES L. SMITH, EDITOR

*you believe in it*
*while you are there*
*because you are there*
*and sometimes you may even feel happy*
*to be that far on your way*
*to somewhere*

M.S. Merwin, "Neither Here nor There"

# Contents

INTRODUCTION
Transport, Scape, Flow: Medieval Transport Systems
*James L. Smith · 13*

↔

*Bios* in the *Prik of Conscience*:
The Apophatic Body and the Sensuous Soul
*Christopher Roman · 19*

*Concordia Discors*: The Traveling Heart as Foreign Object in Chaucer's *Troilus and Criseyde*
*Jennie Friedrich · 35*

*Whan I schal passyn hens*:
Moving With/In *The Book of Margery Kempe*
*Robert Stanton · 53*

Animal Vehicles: Mobility beyond Metaphor
*Carolynn Van Dyke · 71*

Building Bridges to Canterbury
*Sarah Breckenridge Wright · 93*

Chaucer's Physics: Motion in *The House of Fame*
*Thomas R. Schneider · 115*

Contributors · 131

INTRODUCTION

# Transport, Scape, Flow
## Medieval Transport Systems

*James L. Smith*

This volume was born in airports, those strange, seemingly-artificial islands of commerce and activity located in remote industrial fringe zones away from the pulsing hubs of our cities. Filled with a contrived form of vitality by thousands of retail staff, businesses, support industries and engineering facilities, these sprawling complexes warp the social spaces that surround them — displacing, yet creating. Within the gleaming halls of these shrines to our peregrinations, the passenger is neither *here* nor *there,* but in a strange state of intermediacy. Airports are a reconfiguration of space and time familiar to all air travellers — particularly to the academic — and yet redolent of phenomena that exist within intriguing corners of literature and history. It is the analogues of these strange twenty-first century experiences, their transits, transports, scapes, and flows, that inspired this collection. These essays follow twisting paths through literature that offer a liminal vantage point on ideas in progress. Like all experiences of being in transit, there is beauty and meaning when conventional movement recedes.

To be an airline passenger in transit is to move through states without permanently adopting them. The very legal nature of a transit lounge embodies this perfectly. When one is in transit, one does not pass through immigration and enter the legal boundaries of a nation-state. The strange nature of transit is best exemplified by its failures — the case of Mehran Karimi Nasseri, for example, who lived in Charles de Gaulle airport Terminal One for 17 years (1988–2006) after leaving Iran. Nasseri was separated from his refugee documentation while in the process of travelling to the UK to claim asylum, and found himself in a legal grey zone. Having legally entered the airport and being unable to legally leave it, his prolonged state of transit became famous, known to many of us through Tom Hanks's character in Steven Spielberg's 2004 film *The Terminal*. Arrested and enabled motions are lenses through which we view the complications of a process that is seamless when viewed *post facto*. Only disruption — be it Nasseri's extreme experience or thoughtful scholarly reflection — reveals the artificiality of completion.

Eileen Joy and I were both drawn to transit lounges as admirers, quasi-spaces so frequently encountered and yet so unusual when compared to other experiences of space and time. This led us to a mutual appreciation of intermediate motions and transitions between states, the flows and conduits proposed by the sociologist John Urry in the articulation of his mobile sociology thesis. In his seminal essay, Urry proposes that

> Scapes are the networks of machines, technologies, organizations, texts and actors that constitute various interconnected nodes along which flows can be relayed. Such scapes reconfigure the dimensions of time and space. Once particular scapes have been established, then individuals and especially corporations within each society will normally try to become connected to them through being constituted as nodes within that particular network.[1]

The appreciation of texts and transits — their establishment, their reconfiguring effect, their myriad reconnections — inspired the title of this volume and its antecedent roundtables at

---

1   John Urry, "Mobile Sociology," *British Journal of Sociology* 51, no. 1 (2000): 185–203, at 193.

the 2014 New Chaucer Society congress in Reykjavik, Iceland. As medievalists at a conference focused upon the age of Chaucer, we and our participants reflected on the manner in which the strange intermediate states, transactions, motions, and emotions of being in a place of transition could be applied to medieval literature. The result of these reflections was a focus on many forms of strange motion, interaction, space, time, and being. As the reader will apprehend from the essays within, the end product of six scholarly wanderings in the transit, transport, scapes, and flows of their subject matter was a passionate engagement with themes of entanglement, embodiment, mobility, and the structures and mechanisms by which medieval literature and medieval minds sought to negotiate them.

The equally problematic and oft-strange complications of transit in a medieval context have proved to be a rich field of study for our contributors. The pre-modern analogue that framed this discussion was the notion of the *thurghfare,* or thoroughfare. In Chaucer's *Knight's Tale* the aged Egeus, learned in "this worldes transmutacioun," offers stoic council to his son Theseus upon the death of Arcite: "This world nis but a thurghfare ful of wo," the old man advises, "and we ben pilgrimes, passinge to and fro."[2] In the manner of the elderly mentor, Egeus reminds us that our lives are ephemeral pilgrimages, and he also points to the idea of the world as a sort of transit system.

The essays within this volume treat medieval texts themselves as transit systems in which we can glimpse the mobility of objects, figures, mentalities, tropes and other "matter" in vibrant intermediate networks. Each piece is a step on a journey, a temporary caesura in the rambling poetry of literary motion, passing from corporeal to abstract, interacting and pausing — yet never reaching "completion." As scholarship should be, they converse rather than conclude. They reflect their subject matter, stopping at a series of ontological sights and vistas as they journey through medieval literature, weaving in and out of familiar

---

2   Chaucer, *The Knight's Tale,* 2847–48, in Larry D. Benson, ed., *The Riverside Chaucer,* 3rd. ed. (Princeton: Houghton Mifflin, 1987), 63.

tropes within the age of Chaucer while also suggesting interactions far beyond their scope. Within the essays, the reader will find seemingly disparate elements of medieval thought fusing together, forming temporary constructs, and dissolving back into endless motion.

Christopher Roman pierces the black box of human corporeality in "*Bios* in the *Prik of Conscience*: The Apophatic Body and the Sensuous Soul," spilling its essence into the wider medieval thought-world and cosmos. Through penitential self-examination, a vibrant and highly permeable membrane emerges, ever in transition.

Jennie Friedrich scrutinises the estrangement of self through peregrinatory spiritual transactions of the heart in "*Concordia Discors*: The Traveling Heart as Foreign Object in Chaucer's Troilus and Criseyde." Her theme of harmonious discord reveals much of the existential mobility of internal space, transacting with external and alien forces, acquiring new and unfamiliar properties and ontologies in exchange.

Robert Stanton reveals the restless transitions of a familiar and yet ever-fruitful text in "*Whan I schal passyn hens*: Moving With/In *The Book of Margery Kempe*," navigating the restless shifting of Margery through space, time, categories, communities, and expressions of authorial intent and identity. These roamings continue to touch and mold twenty-first-century scholarship and pedagogy, shaping our experience of the text.

Carolynn Van Dyke details the ceaseless mobility of the animal as a site of meaning and expression of agency in "Animal Vehicles: Mobility beyond Metaphor." Her essay navigates agriculture, zoology, bestiary, theology to reveal ontological and literary restlessness. Etymological and ecological webs defy cultural homogenisation and reach beyond symbolism and metaphor to the shared ties of lively, ceaseless matter.

Sarah Breckenridge Wright journeys to the Blissful Martyr by a path less travelled in "Building Bridges to Canterbury." Bridging spaces of landscape, literature, and identity, her essay simultaneously encounters disruptions to travel, experiencing the practical and abstract dimensions of medieval bridge building. Through a Chaucerian lens, we see the locus of the bridge itself as a site of unique identity and resonance.

Thomas R. Schneider follows the motion of medieval literature and physics in "Chaucer's Physics: Motion in *The House of Fame*," taking the reader to a world permeated by Ockhamism and Aristotelianism as explained by a didactic eagle. The lessons marry the dynamism of natural philosophy and literature: motion narrated in motion, the motion of medieval rules, the journey of medieval literature, and the three forming a tangle of diverse, moving forces, literary physics in motion.

Many thanks are due to those who have contributed their own special touches to this volume. First of all to the contributors: their ceaseless enthusiasm for their subject matter, set into motion by a pre-publication sharing and synthesising of ideas that was inspirational to behold. To Eileen Joy, for co-chairing the NCS roundtables that generated this volume, for supporting this volume, and for all of her powerful and effective work at punctum books. To the punctum team: Chris Piuma for his wonderful cover, Vincent W.J. van Gerven Oei for making it all come together, and Matt Ossias for his close and precise editing. To the NCS presenters who do not appear within these pages, but who helped to shape the volume through their excellent papers shared in Reykjavik: Louise Bishop, Gaelan Gilbert, Sealy Gilles, Katherine Koppelman, Sarah Novacich, Steele Nowlin, and Nicholas Perkins. Finally, a big thank you to the reader, who is supporting independent and open access publishing by reading this volume.

1

# *Bios* in the *Prik of Conscience*
## The Apophatic Body and the Sensuous Soul

*Christopher Roman*

I.

In his 1981–82 lectures entitled *The Hermeneutics of the Subject,* Michel Foucault formulates that in the process of the self coming to truth in spirituality, the subject must be "changed, transformed, shifted, and, become, to some extent and up to a certain point, other than himself."[1] This paper thinks with the *Prik of Conscience* (c. 1400)[2] as it presents the reader and penitent with the problem of the self as it becomes "other than" itself. This process of becoming other than oneself is reflected in the idea of the penitent as a pilgrim passing through worlds. On the one hand, the unknown author of the *Prik of Conscience* is concerned with exploring "the more world," or the macrocosm, and its connection with "the less world," the microcosm. On the other hand,

---

1 Michel Foucault, *The Hermeneutics of the Subject: Lectures at the College de France, 1981–82,* ed. Frederic Gross, trans. Graham Burchell (New York: Picador, 2001), 15.
2 All citations from the *Prik of Conscience,* ed. James H. Morey (Kalamazoo: Medieval Institute Publications, 2012). The *Prik of Conscience* is anonymous, therefore I use the designation "*Conscience*-author" following the pattern of other anonymous medieval works such as *The Cloud of Unknowing* and *Cloud*-author.

the *Conscience*-author is concerned with a kind of life, what the Greeks referred to as *bios,* linked with self-examination in the process of penitence.³ The penitential self-examination is linked to the relationship between macrocosm and microcosm. The penitent must find a way to unsay the self in order to become connected with these two iterations of cosmos.

As the *Conscience*-author formulates, in order to know of God: "hymselfe he mot know withinne" (Entre, 138).⁴ The *Prik of Conscience* is a document outlining a "technology of self": in this case, Foucault's formulation of an exomologesis, defined as "the dramatic recognition of one's status as a penitent."⁵ This dramatic recognition occurs in the *Prik of Conscience* within an apophaticism of the body. Unsaying the body undoes the "itself" in order to see the radical incompatibility in the self's understanding of body as it works in only one aspect of the cosmos, the microcosm. This unsaying in turn dissolves the penitent's false relation to a concept of world sensed through a body conditioned by economic and social structures while rethinking relations with the cosmos in which they travel. The *Prik of Conscience* suggests a penitential practice that finds God by exploring the body's implication in the relationships to these worlds.

---

3   For an analysis of the conflation of *zoē* and *bios* see Giorgio Agamben, *Homo Sacer: Sovereign Power and Bare Life,* trans. Daniel Heller-Roazen (Stanford: Stanford University Press, 1998).

4   For a discussion of the manuscripts evolution and importance in medieval parish culture, see Robert E. Lewis and Angus McIntosh, *A Descriptive Guide to the Manuscripts of the Prick of Conscience* (Oxford: Society for the Study of Medieval Language and Literature, 1982). For a lexigraphical interpretation of *The Prick of Conscience* see Maria José Carillo-Linares's "Interpreting and Mapping Raw Data for Middle English Word Geography: The Case of *The Prick of Conscience,*" *Neuphilologische Mitteilungen* 11, no. 3 (2010): 321–44. Further lexigraphical interpretation can be found in Angus McIntosh's "Two Unnoticed Interpolations in Four Manuscripts of *The Prick of Conscience,*" *Neuphilologische Mitteilungen* 77 (1976): 63–78.

5   Michel Foucault, "Technologies of the Self," in *Technologies of the Self: A Seminar with Michel Foucault,* eds. Luther H. Martin, Huck Gutman, and Patrick H. Hutton (Amherst: University of Massachusetts Press, 1988), 41.

## II.

The penitent expresses a specific kind of project of individual religious life in the Middle Ages. This essay seeks to think about penitence as a way of life that challenged concepts of being-in-the-world[6] that necessarily always eschew a singular world. Traditionally, the *Prik of Conscience* is categorized as a text in the *contemptus mundi* tradition. Yet, the *Conscience*-author was very concerned with linking the penitential body to wider and wider scales of the universe. It is difficult to take the *Conscience*-author at face-value in terms of contempt while they are exploring and, seemingly celebrating, the nature of the world, though they do denigrate particularly human failings in that world. The *Conscience*-author chides the penitent to do better by expanding the self beyond the body.

In order to move beyond the boundaries of the body, the penitent must unsay the self within two strains of discourse regarding Christian life. As mentioned, Michel Foucault identifies one of these as *exomologesis*. On the one hand the penitent strove to continually verbalize their thinking within confession (*exomologesis*), what Nikolas Rose calls rendering "oneself truthfully into discourse."[7] The other strain is *exagouresis*. *Exagouresis* involves the role of the penitent as in exile from God. Thus, they also work to sacrifice that self. This purgatorial exile reflects what Foucault understood as the way the penitent must "sacrifice the self in order to discover the truth about selves, and have to discover the truth about selves in order to sacrifice selves."[8] This recursive relationship works to create a complex penitential identity that proves boundary-less in order to free itself to be more fully realized in the macrocosm.

---

6  See Martin Heidegger, *Being and Time,* trans. John Macquarrie and Edward Robinson (New York: Harper & Row, 1962).

7  Nikolas Rose, *Governing the Soul: The Shaping of the Private Self,* 2nd ed. (London: Fress Association, 1999), 222.

8  Michel Foucault, "About the Beginning of the Hermeneutics of the Self," in *Religion and Culture: Michel Foucault,* ed. Jeremy Carette (New York: Routledge, 1999), 179.

This recursive relationship comes to fruition within the discourse of confession. As Andrew Galloway has written, the *Prik of Conscience* "stands squarely in the world of real confession that constituted so central a cultural concern in late medieval England."[9] The process of real confession in the *Prik of Conscience,* however, presents the reader with a language of unsaying the body as a move of penitence. To confess, to account for oneself, undoes the self, in this case a self that enacts sin, and also opens the body to other possibilities. The *Prik of Conscience* enacts an apophatical penitential process by contemplating the material body tracing, as the *Conscience*-author writes, "mon" to "un mon" (First Part, 536–537). Apophaticism, then, muddies the easy divide between *bios* and *thanatos* around the body-soul relationship in order to re-imagine being within this text. As John Caputo formulates it in terms of the doctrine of the risen body of Christ, "it is not exactly an affirmation of the body, but of life, and not exactly of life but of a certain life, that is, life without death [...] a simply impossible body."[10] Part of the *Prik of Conscience*'s appeal is the author's ambivalent preference for continually returning to the tension between body and life, and thinking-through a *bios* of a sensuous soul, an impossible, porous thing, rather than meditating on an "external" divinity.

The penitent, then, must see the body both as it has been conditioned by the anthropocentric but also how it is in relation to mico-and macroworlds. As Moira Fitzgibbons and Howard Chickering note, the *Prik of Conscience* is "unalleviatedly tactile."[11] This tactility is related to seeing as a sensual method, a *technē* that the *Conscience*-author employs for ontological un-

---

9   Andrew Galloway, "Gower's *Confessio Amantis,* the *Prick of Consience,* and the History of the Latin Gloss in Early English Literature," in *John Gower: Manuscripts, Readers, Contexts,* ed. Malte Urban, 39–70 (Turnout: Brepols, 2009), 43.
10  John Caputo, "Bodies Still Unrisen, Events Still Unsaid: A Hermeneutic of Bodies without Flesh," in *Apophatic Bodies: Negative Theology, Incarnation, and Relationality,* eds. Catherine Keller and Chris Boesel, 73–86 (New York: Fordham University Press, 2009), 98.
11  Moira Fitzgibbons, "Enabled and Disabled 'Myndes' in 'The Prick of Conscience,'" in *Medieval Poetics and Social Practice: Responding to the Work of*

derstanding of that which transcends the finite self. To bring the body out, to "yeelde" it, this is the prick of conscience, "the deciphering of self."[12] This is also the shock of the sacred — that which resists assimilation to an everydayness.[13] The scopic "processe" (Entre, 225) leads the penitent to a new *kind* of seeing. Bodily seeing is too myopic since the human "love nought bot that they se" (Entre, 285). As Eugene Thacker posits, however, "life is not itself contained with the set that it conditions."[14] How to see and love life beyond this anthropomorphic conditioning? The *Conscience*-author employs "seeing" in many registers. Seeing is understanding. Seeing is knowing. Seeing is truth — these are all examples of Foucault's dramatic recognition. Mirrors, ironically, appear throughout the *Prik of Conscience,* not as symbols of vanity or narcissism, rather, they are used as a way to challenge the traditional scope of anthropomorphic seeing.

Mirrors provide an important scopic tool in the understanding of the nature of divine knowledge. For example, in the Seventh Part of the *Conscience* discussing the joys of heaven, the *Conscience*-author writes that the penitent will see God as one sees in a mirror. Seeing is linked with knowledge, as the penitent will learn how God is both divine and human; how the human fits with God's divinity; and, finally, under the manner of being itself, "all men and thinges les and more" (Seventh Part, 657–660). This kind of knowledge is connected to the way the penitent looks in the mirror and sees themselves in the mirror. The perspective that the *Conscience*-author invites the penitent to entertain not only involves seeing the object of reflection itself — the mirror as object is agentially important in understanding knowledge. The penitent is to see their face and "lykenes" and, as well, that which is reflected besides the peni-

---

    *Penn R. Szittya,* ed. Seeta Chaganti, 72–94 (New York: Fordham University Press, 2012), 75.

12  Nikolas Rose, *Governing the Soul: The Shaping of the Private Self,* 2nd ed. (London: Free Association, 1999), 245.

13  John McSweeney, "Religion in the Web of Immanence: Foucault and Thinking Otherwise after the Death of God," *Foucault Studies* 15 (2013): 72–94.

14  Eugene Thacker, *After Life* (Chicago: University of Chicago Press, 2010), 87.

tent themselves. The mirror is not merely a reflecting tool or an invitation to narcissistic admiration of the self; rather, the mirror becomes a figure of divine seeing. The connection between the penitent and the mirror allows the world that is reflected to become a part of the penitent's being. The mirror's scopic power arranges the penitent so that they see divinely, the reflection itself frees the penitent from anthropomorphic thinking into a wider world. The mirror is capable of "seeing" way more than the penitent can on their own. As well, penitential seeing mirrors Jesus' judgmental gaze at the end of the world; that which is "inner" — the conscience, the soul, forgotten deeds — is no longer contained by the body, but stands before the penitent, making the account, the truth, undeniable. The penitent sees themselves at that moment as God would. It is this model of seeing that must be used in this world; the penitent becomes the image of Jesus.

As with the mirror, the *Conscience*-author experiments with non-human seeing to connect microcosm with macrocosm. Employing the figure of the lynx, an animal that "may se thorowe thicke ston walles" (First Part, 204), the *Conscience*-author argues that if the penitent could see inside of their bodies, or see it from below, or even take a birds-eye view of the body, that they would see the body as more than its "set." As Jennie Friedlich indicates in this volume, the body becomes a site for "openness and violability." By dismantling anthropomorphic seeing, the penitent recognizes the strangeness of the body and how the body supercedes the macrocosm.[15] To see oneself as truth is seeing the body as world: as the *Conscience*-author describes, "askes, poudur, erthe, and clay" (First Part, 55) — these are the matter of the body as much as they are of the world. It is worth noting here, as well, that the body is linked to the four elements (ashes: fire, powder: air; earth: earth; clay: water). The body is porous, mediated by elements, implicated with matter.

As the *Conscience*-author indicates, "this worlde is way and passage / wherby we make oure pilgrimage / by this way mote we

---

15 Ibid., 87.

iwis" (Second Part, 449–451). The penitent is a pilgrim carefully picking their way through the world-as-bridge. Love, dread, and humility are the terms that the penitent must balance, but it is important to note that the *Prik of Conscience* does not fit neatly into the penitential genre; there are no recommendations *for* penance, just that one must *be* penitent.[16] This *technē* of penitence is found within a love-dread-humility matrix in which the body must see itself for what it is: an apophatic body; a body that is *not* since it is always already undoing.

An apophatic body, however, is also an embodied identity. As Catherine Keller and Chris Boesel point out, "the traditional apophatic gesture negated our bodied finitude only inasmuch as finite forms are mistaken for the divine infinite."[17] The Pseudo-Dionysus warns against this mistake when he writes that *The Mystical Theology* is not for those who "imagine that there is nothing beyond instances of individual being."[18] The *Conscience*-author underscores this by equating soul with life and life with God. Sin is one kind of dying, since "the soule sleyn withinne" (Third Part, 47) and God refuses to dwell there. But, penance can make the soul "hole within" (Third Part, 60). If the body is always being unsaid in order to see its finitude, the soul is constantly resurrected to rethink its divine irreducibility.

By meditating on the body in its processes in his descriptions, the *Conscience*-author posits the body's superabundance. The *Conscience*-author employs, as Thacker writes, an "overflowing negation that posits, in a contradictory way, the continuity that is also our own non-human limit. To exist as the world, we must cease existing *in* the world."[19] The *Conscience*-author directs us

---

16 For a discussion of penitentials and their connection to the institutionalization of penance see Talal Asad, *Genealogies of Religion: Disciple and Reasons of Power in Christianity and Islam* (Baltimore: Johns Hopkins University Press, 1993).
17 Catherine Keller and Chris Boesel, "Introduction," in *Apophatic Bodies: Negative Theology, Incarnation, and Relationality,* eds. Catherine Keller and Chris Boesel, 1–24 (New York: Fordham University Press, 2009), 4.
18 Pseudo-Dionysus, *The Mystical Theology,* trans. Colm Luibheid (New York: Paulist Press, 1987), 136
19 Eugene Thacker, *In the Dust of the Planet* (Winchester: Zero, 2011), 149.

to look at this overflowing negation: "yif a mon myght se his synne / in kynde a lykenesse that he is inne / for fere he shulde sonner it fle" (Third Part, 626–628). The scopic process undoes the sin from the sinner; in its external embodiment it is recognized. A penitential *bios* returns an understanding of the body as cosmos by relegating sin to a being only bound to a world. Sin is far *too* human.

The *Conscience*-author's conception of cosmos is anti-creation in so far as it is connected to the merely anthropocentric. Despite his devotion to hundreds of lines over the doomsday signs and the burning of the world, so that by the end of the Fifth Part the judged and renewed world "shineth as clear as is cristalle" (2212), Books One through Four continually wrestle with body and world. For example, during the discussion of the muck that is the body, the *Conscience*-author celebrates how herbs bring forth seeds and trees bring forth fruit, while the human body brings forth pests: "nytes, fleen, lyus, and vermyn" (First Part, 274). By placing the body in this botanical taxonomy, the *Conscience*-author suggests that the body is merely an upside-down tree, or that instead of fruit, the human brings forth and is afflicted by innumerable diseases. By seeing self in humility as vegetable, the penitent sees themselves bound to the world, not apart from it. If olives bring olive oil, and grapes can produce wine, the human manufacturing of spit and vomit (First Part, 278) proves human effluvia as worthy of *humilitas*. Further, as the *Conscience*-author implores in his meditation on the heavenly bodies: "the bodyes therof in her kynde / us shewen ensaumple to have in mynde / to serve God in our kynde here / As they doon there in her manere" (Second Part, 93–96). That is to implore, why can the penitent not be more like a star? There is a certain beauty in this observation; seeing themselves as plant or cosmic matter invites penitents to see themselves as *part* of creation, rather than apart from it.

The *Conscience*-author, then, explores the cosmos through penitential seeing and suggests that the world has been understood only through the lens of "worldly men."[20] The *Conscience*-author then asks, "what myght men by worlde undurstond / Yif no mon were therin wonand?" (Second Part, 141–142). The problem of world is that the penitent sees it through the filter of those who love a certain configured world too much, and the reader has to parse the *Conscience*-author further: it's *this* world (Second Part, 155) — it's the impersonal pronoun that defines a world that "worldly men" have made out of whack with a larger cosmography. As well, the *Conscience*-author indicates that "als this worldes vanytee / They woold noon othur world se" (Second Part, 666–667). Here he separates the problem of "this" world as not the only world; however, it is the only world the sinful is able to comprehend or "se."

It is also in this Part that the *Conscience*-author explains the problem of "the worldes mannere" (Second Part, 164). The *Conscience*-author spends over one hundred lines critiquing wealth and how the worldly celebrate being "over-bysy" (Second Part, 162). The problem ultimately is that humanity renders themselves as slaves to a world that they have exiled themselves within (Second Part, 222). By posing the question of a world without *this* kind of humanity, the *Conscience*-author asks the reader to then imagine the penitential self as a self in a perpetual state of becoming, never static, permeating ever new modes of being in a shifting world.

As Jeremy Carette writes, "the discourse of spirituality at least opens up the politics of continual transformation by holding up what we can be and what is not yet seen."[21] The scopic, for Carette, is implicit in new possibilities contained within the spiritual. The *Conscience*-author is pointing to the way the spiritual can unfold new possibilities, a way to unlock a new visual

---

20 For a discussion of the link between rationality and mind, see Fitzgibbons, "Enabled and Disabled 'Myndes' in *The Prick of Conscience*"; Howell Chickering, "Rhetorical Stimulus in the Prick of Conscience," in *Medieval Paradigms: Essays in Honor of Jeremy duQuesnay Adams,* ed. Stephanie Hayes-Healy, 2 vols., 1:191–230 (New York: Palgrave Macmillan, 2005).

21 Jeremy Carette, "Rupture and Transformation: Foucault's Concept of Spirituality Reconsidered," *Foucault Studies* 15 (2013): 52–71, at 71.

spectrum and see the human body in new ways. As others have argued, confession is a way to reveal oneself,[22] but it is also a way to "unfold God in our bodies [...] this is an 'I' precisely not as separate or autonomous ego but us as one among all the creatures participating at every moment in each other."[23] What is remarkable about the *Conscience*-author's version of Purgatory is how porous it is with the living, revealing how it participates in life. Penitence and Purgatory touch the world in ways that the body affects and is affected by. Purgatory is a state and a place that affects the soul across time and space shaping a *bios* of the living and the dead. In other words, to use Giorgio Agamben's formulation of monastic exile, *this* is a Purgatorial world, a non-monastic exile, shaping "a new community and a new public sphere."[24]

As Foucault formulates it, the penitent's confession is akin to "the relation to the truth [as] established in the form of a face-to-face relationship with God and in a human confidence with corresponds to the effusion of divine love" that is indicative of the penitential tradition.[25] In this forging of penitential identity, and in the demands of the face-to-face encounter, the *Conscience*-author is remapping a Christian body in terms of Foucault's positive *parrhēsia*. In turn, Adam Kotsko argues that we need to think about the human differently:

---

22 See Talal Asad, "Pain and Truth in Medieval Christian Ritual," especially the discussion of relation between penitence and purgatory in terms of medicine for the soul, 103.
23 Catherine Keller, "The Cloud of the Impossible: Embodiment and Apophasis," in *Apophatic Bodies: Negative Theology, Incarnation, and Relationality*, eds. Catherine Keller and Chris Boesel, 25–44 (New York: Fordham University Press, 2009), 42.
24 Giorgio Agamben, *The Highest Poverty: Monastic Rules and Form-of-Life*, trans. Adam Kotsko (Stanford: Stanford University Press, 2013), 50.
25 Michel Foucault, "28 March 1984: Second Hour," *The Courage of Truth: The Government of Self and Others II, Lectures at the College de France 1983–1984*, ed. Frédéric Gross, trans. Graham Burchell (New York: Palgrave Macmillan, 2011), 337.

Humanity stands at a nodal point in the universe, at a nexus of rich variety of relationships. This is true at the level of the individual, as the patristic authors attempted to indicate by their rejections of a monadic soul and their insistence that the human being is the relationship between body and soul — that is, even the individual is relational 'all the way down.' But my core principal means that the body and soul can't be conceived as two inert things that happen to be in relationship to each other. Instead, they are themselves singularities emerging from a network of relationships.[26]

The *Conscience*-author unlocks scopic possibility in order to unlock Kotsko's "network of relationships": if we could see the body

> fro above and fro bynethe
> mich fylthe and stynkyng brethe.
> More stynke is non harden ny nessh
> Then the filthe of monns flesshe
> That may a mon both se and fele
> Yif he beholde hymselven wele (Book One, 238–244)

The penitent is misled by not taking account of the *whole* body and the way it works in the microcosm.[27] For the *Conscience*-author, the body is always framed by what the reader has been conditioned to see by the hermeneutic of the world's vanities, not a realist ontology that reveals the greater worlds. In the case of the *Prik of Conscience,* in taking account of unsaying the body, the whole stinking, vermin-infested, and deconstructing biome leads the penitent to see the truth.

The *Conscience*-author's world reveals how the worldly have twisted it through not *seeing* it. We can see the *Conscience*-au-

---

26 Adam Kotsko, *The Politics of Redemption: The Social Logic of Salvation* (New York: Bloomsbury Academic, 2010), 189.

27 For an analysis of the corpse as a heterogeneous object, dead to itself, but food for others, see Karl Steel, "Abyss: Everything is Food," *postmedieval: a journal of medieval cultural studies* 4 (2013): 93–104.

thor's exploration of life in the world when he critiques what we have made of the world. If God's creation is "good," and made for our profit, then what does profit even mean? Environments are twisted by the human: the sea is a symbol for changeableness; the wilderness is full of animals that bite as do "tyrants and misdoers" (Second Part, 286); the forest is full of people who rob us; the field is a *battle* field; and the macrocosm has two hands holding happiness and woe, both of which are tied to wealth, again, which the human, in turn, has given a twisted shape. If the body is misunderstood then, fundamentally, so is this world. To die well, this kind of world must, too, be unsaid.

Parts One and Two reveal a body in the matrix of love, humility and dread which opens the penitent to, as Keller and Boesel write, "dimensions of embodiment that cannot be reduced to biological, sociological, or for that matter theological abstraction without again confusing the abstract with the concrete."[28] The sinner dreads what they do not see; they do not see because we only see anthropomorphically. In this way, the *Conscience*-author has prepared the penitent to give an account of their life.

In giving an account, one must divide up life into categories: time, deeds, and behaviors are all necessary for the accounting. This making visible of ones' life is clear in the *Conscience*-author's discussion of the final judgment in which those things that are internal, such as conscience or sins that have not been repented enough, stand and accuse — again, an example of Foucault's dramatic recognition.[29] The penitent sees themselves projected before their eyes. In the *Conscience*-author's language one must "streyte acounte yelde" (Fifth Part, 1577) of various aspects of life. This "yeelde" is a giving over. Or, as Jean-Luc Nancy formulates, faith's ability to "open the world in itself to its own outside."[30] The self is too insular — confession and accounting

---

28 Keller and Boesel, "Introduction," 7.

29 For a discussion of the *Prik of Conscience*'s influence on modern literature see Roy K. Bird, "'Agenbite of Inwit': *Prick of Conscience,* Sting of Command in James Joyce's *Ulysses*," *North Dakota Quarterly* 51, no. 4 (1983): 68–79.

30 Jean-Luc Nancy, *Dis-Enclosure: The Deconstruction of Christianity,* trans. Bettina Bergo, Gabriel Malenant, and Michael B. Smith (New York: Ford-

allow the human to see its exteriors which are normally hidden from them.

Revealing the hidden is an important aspect of accounting for a capacious, ultimately, and admittedly, only partial self. As Judith Butler writes, "my account of myself is partial, haunted by that for which I can devise no definitive story."[31] The ghosts of Purgatory haunt our account of ourselves — as in the medieval Purgatory poem, *Gast of Gy,* what the penitent cannot, will not, or is unable to account for comes back to them. Purgatory is a haunting: it is within the earth (common) and above the earth someplace (special).[32] The body forgets, the soul remembers. The first pains of Purgatory have to do with the dread over the soul and body's separation and the judgment of the soul. These two haunting anxieties mimic concerns over the living's death. Even after one has died, the soul is still worried about these same problems. The *Conscience*-author's worry may be tagged as "have I represented myself fully?" There will be resolution only in the final judgment. Perhaps, realizing this, the *Conscience*-author recommends methods of living that will help both the living and those in Purgatory. There is nothing one can do for those in Heaven or Hell. Prayers to those who are damned help lessen the numbers in Hell, and in Heaven bring some extra joy (maybe), but in Purgatory prayer assists those to proceed through their Purgatory quicker, in lessening their pain. The efficacy of prayer is mostly for those who are alive in the world and the Purgatorial appointed.

---

ham University Press, 2008), 2.

31 Judith Butler, *Giving and Account of Oneself* (New York: Fordham University Press, 2005), 40.

32 For an analysis of Middle English purgatorial poems focusing on the grey area of place and state, see Robert Easting, "Send Thine Heart Into Purgatory: Visionaries of the Other World," in *The Long Fifteenth Century: Essays for Douglas Gray,* eds. Helen Cooper and Sally Mapstone, 185–204 (Oxford: Clarendon, 1997).

## III.

The ethic that the *Conscience*-author is concerned with is how the penitent undoes the self and is ethically obligated to help the souls in other worlds. The soul's body is full of affect, but there is a gravity to the soul, dragging it down. Penitence allows the penitent to levitate, to be more like stars. But, Purgatory is also a state, it touches the earth after all. It is a ghost of the world; the seventh pain of Purgatory, in fact, is being exposed to the wilderness. In order to circumnavigate the wilderness and the pain, both for oneself and for the dead, is to enact certain behaviors, to overcome sin: the use of holy water, alms, fasting, taking Communion, praying the Our Father, confession, blessings by the authorities, knocking of the breast, and anointing of the sick. These various *technai* reveal the capabilities of the penitential body and help it disrupt venial sins, *this* world. This is making the body a body that touches the divine; it is a making of the body to live "in this world and equally as physically in the world to come." [33]

For the *Conscience*-author venial sin is social sin; his accounting of venial sins reveal Foucault's evolving body. Do not drink or eat too much, do not speak sharply to the poor, do not eat when one is already full and should be fasting, do not sleep too late and miss church, do not pray half-heartedly, do not have sex without intending procreation, do not, do not, do not. This ever-evolving penitential body will assist in skipping the pains of Purgatory so the accounting at the Day of Judgment will be more fluid. But it also suggests a way to *live* well — to be concerned with oneself as it is stretched across multiverses.

As the *Conscience*-author concludes, in an overly-positive register considering where we have been in previous chapters, God will "bring hitte to that blysful place / where joy evere is and eke solace, / to the whiche place he is alle bryng" (Seventh

---

33 Graham Ward, "The Metaphysics of the Body," in *Apophatic Bodies: Negative Theology, Incarnation, and Relationality,* eds. Catherine Keller and Chris Boesel, 227–50 (New York: Fordham University Press, 2009), 248.

Part, 1942–1944). Considering the imagined rendering of those who are damned and saved, the "all" underscores the forgiveness which the sinner makes through the continual undoing of self in this ever evolving account.

The practice of Penitence and its vibrations found in the touch of Purgatory, then, manage *bios*. The body is unsaid: it decays and disperses, yet its relationship with the sensuous soul is managed through purgatorial practice. Hell and Heaven are here in terms of punishment and reward, but those are less complex in terms of guiding the penitence in ethical living. It is the Purgatorial body, the body in process that reveals life to be one of a duty to worlds. The enactment of various *technai* forces the penitent to acknowledge the dust of the cosmos in themselves, as well as the way that the inability to fully account for the self is a way to mark the ways that the self is part of bigger and bigger spheres of worlds. In Judith Butler's phrasing "the failure to narrate fully may well indicate the way in which we are from the start, ethically implicated in the lives of others."[34] Purgatorial space exists as a palimpsest, a bare membrane, in which the constantly unsaying body touches the sensuous soul. The penitent lives in fluid membranes, ever-stretching, as they work to move the body and soul beyond its capabilities into overflowing and boundless worlds.

---

34  Butler, *Giving an Account of Oneself*, 64.

2

# *Concordia Discors*
# The Traveling Heart as Foreign Object in Chaucer's *Troilus and Criseyde*

Jennie Friedrich

*Quid velit et possit rerum concordia discors.*
— Horace, *Epistles* I:xii, l. 4[1]

### Interior Landscapes of the Body and their Implications

The quote from Horace's *Epistles* in my epigraph succinctly articulates the complexity of the heart's physical movements and characteristics in Chaucer's *Troilus and Criseyde*: what I will discuss in this essay as a process of *concordia discors,* or harmonious discord. Hearts in this poem are sometimes just symbols, particularly in the frequent references to Troilus's heartache.[2] In other instances, hearts are profoundly material, and even objectified in very specific and consistent ways throughout the narrative. This essay focuses on the removal and exchange of disembodied and objectified hearts, their profound effects on

---

1 [What would and could result from the harmonious discord of things.] See Horace, *Epistles* (London: ECCO–York University, 1746).
2 For more on the symbolic function of the hearts in Troilus and Criseyde more generally, see S.L. Clark and Julian N. Wasserman, "The Heart in *Troilus and Criseyde*: The Eye of the Breast, the Mirror of the Mind, The Jewel in its Setting," *The Chaucer Review* 18, no. 4 (1984): 316–28.

notions of identity and ontological integrity in the poem. The interactions between hearts and bodies in *Troilus and Criseyde* also create a complex interplay of transits, transports, scapes,[3] and flows. Bodies move, but they are also at times transported against their will. Hearts are sometimes part of the internal landscapes of bodies, but at other times they are transported out of bodies. While the degree to which physical dynamics governing movement and physical integrity in works of fantasy remains a subject of critical debate, I argue that Chaucer's insistence on materiality — that the hearts function in material ways that align them with their cultural function — grants the traveling hearts some degree of scientific gravitas within their historical context.[4] The dual function of the heart, as both a vessel and a thing to be placed inside a vessel, makes it the ideal representation for the cultural conflicts of the Trojan War as represented in Chaucer's poem. Themes of invasion, mobility, and displacement are pivotal to the plot, and encapsulated by the material forms and movements of the eagle's heart and the heart-shaped ruby brooch in the poem. For this reason, I will focus on the ways in which the forms of cognitive estrangement present in this poem — alienation of the reader from his or her physical reality through cognitive organization of an alternate reality — engage with the physical environment of the body, its interior, and the organization thereof.

---

3   John Urry, "Mobile Sociology," *British Journal of Sociology* 51, no. 1 (2000): 185–203.

4   For the original argument reserving the notion of cognitive estrangement for strictly science fiction texts, see Darko Suvin, *Metamorphoses of Science Fiction: On the Poetics and History of a Literary Genre* (New Haven: Yale University Press, 1979). For an argument in favor of dismantling the generic "firewall" between science fiction and fantasy, see Mark Bould and China Miéville, *Red Planets* (Middletown: Wesleyan University Press, 2009), 231. Carl Freedman argues that scientific realism is dependent on a narrative's historical context. For more on this, see *Critical Theory and Science Fiction* (Middletown: Wesleyan University Press, 2000), 43. Finally, Adam Charles Roberts argues that the affective power of the "science" in science fiction lies in the tension between cognition and estrangement or alienation in the concept of "cognitive estrangement." See *Science Fiction: the New Critical Idiom* (London and New York: Routledge, 2006), 8.

This essay is organized according to three physical realities of medieval travel described by Jean Verdon:

> [Travel] had so little substance that at first it was identified with the concrete elements that made it up: the road itself (*via* — way or journey), or the money needed to carry it out (*viaticum*). Later came the sense of movement, especially as carried out by pilgrims, and then by those armed pilgrims, the crusaders.[5]

The main concerns of territory, exchange, and movement described by Verdon reveal the importance of thinking through the *internal* landscapes transformed by travel. As Verdon implies, movement across vast landscapes mattered less to the medieval definition of travel than the suffering and loss incurred by the traveler on the journey. Medieval travelers were likely to be robbed or killed on the roads. They had to travel through dense forests and uncharted landscapes, which introduces the threats of misdirection and disorientation into the structure of bodily damage in medieval travel literature. In light of this understanding of travel, it makes sense to talk about medieval travel in material and microcosmic ways. Movement across vast landscapes matters less to the medieval definition of travel than the suffering and loss incurred on the journey. Bodies are the primary territories in question. Finally, the financial cost of travel mentioned in Verdon's description is also useful for making sense of the exchanges in the narrative, and it too becomes a question of bodily movement and damage in the poem. Although literal currency is not a concern in *Troilus and Criseyde*, systems of exchange involving hearts and bodies are integral to processes of disorientation and estrangement, particularly when the body or heart being exchanged is incapacitated or stripped of agency — and thereby objectified — or when the exchange is involuntary.

---

5 Jean Verdon, *Travel in the Middle Ages* (Notre Dame: University of Notre Dame Press, 2003), 1.

Using these methods for categorizing the concrete elements of medieval travel, in this essay I reframe the familiar medieval trope of the disembodied heart in *Troilus and Criseyde*, employing theories of incorporation to examine how the movements of the hearts in this narrative actually reflect and threaten the unstable identities of the characters.[6] In addition to the distinct functions of estrangement and foreignness in the poem, two medieval literary manifestations of the heart are also vital. The first is examined in Heather Webb's study of medical and metaphorical conceptions of the heart in literature and culture.[7] The second, the relationship between the heart and the "metaphor of the inner person or self as a kind of text," is explored in Eric Jager's *The Book of the Heart*.[8] The power structure in *Troilus and Criseyde* is based on foreignness, allegiance, and acculturation, which alters the figurative landscape. The treatment of hearts, bodies, and movements emphasizes the internalization of foreign objects. Troilus, meaning "Little Troy," is the human embodiment of the city of Troy, which renders his fate inextricable from that of the city. Early in Book 1, the arrogant Troilus mocks the pain of lovers and the "God of Love" shoots him with an arrow:

> And with that word he gan caste up the browe,
> Ascaunces, "Loo! Is this naught wisely spoken?"
> At which the God of Love gan loken rowe
> Right for despit, and shop for to ben wroken.
> He kidde anon his bowe nas naught broken;
> For sodeynly he hitte hym atte fulle —

---

6   The heart reflects identity in that it is recognizable as belonging to the body, but it threatens the integrity of the body and its identity when it is removed from the body. Conversely, a heart that does not belong to the body, when inserted into the body, is foreign and therefore threatening.

7   Heather Webb, *The Medieval Heart* (New Haven and London: Yale University Press, 2010).

8   Eric Jager, *The Book of the Heart* (Chicago: University of Chicago Press, 2001).

And yet as proud a pekok kan he pulle. (1:204–210)⁹

From this point forward, Troilus begins to desire Criseyde.¹⁰ In this tale, Criseyde's uncle, Pandarus, acts as the mediator between the two lovers. Love is largely absent from the narrative, except as an abstract influence on the characters. Pandarus makes a number of overwrought speeches to Criseyde about how Troilus will die if she does not love him, and finally, Criseyde begins to fall in love. Soon after, however, Criseyde discovers that her traitorous father, now living in Greece, has orchestrated a trade in which she will be sent to Greece in exchange for the imprisoned Trojan warrior Antenor. Troilus begs Criseyde to remain faithful to him, but Criseyde ultimately transfers her allegiance to Diomede:

> Soone after this they spake of sondry thynges,
> As fel to purpos of this aventure,
> And pleyinge entrechaungeden hire rynges,
> Of whiche I kan nought tellen no scripture;
> But wel I woot, a broche, gold and asure,
> In which a ruby was set lik an herte,
> Criseyde hym yaf, and stak it on his sherte. (III:1366–1372)

According to *The Aeneid*, when Antenor returns to Troy, he betrays the Trojans by letting the Trojan horse into the city.¹¹

Drawing also upon Stephen Greenblatt's theory of "estrangement-effect," which states that geographical and cultural strangeness alienate the traveler, I argue that the figure of the

---

9 *Troilus and Criseyde* in Larry D. Benson, ed., *The Riverside Chaucer*, 3rd. ed. (Princeton: Houghton Mifflin, 1987). Hereafter cited parenthetically by book and line number.

10 This allies the structure of desire here more closely with Cavalcanti than with Dante, but Cavalcanti's darts are shot from the lady's eyes through the lover's eyes and into his heart, whereas Cupid simply shoots Troilus with an arrow here, the story giving the reader no indication of whether it reached Troilus's heart.

11 *A Companion to the Aeneid and Its Tradition*, eds. Joseph Farrell and Michael C.J. Putnam (Oxford: Wiley-Blackwell, 2010), 137–38.

heart serves as the symbolic physical manifestation of that distance that foreignness creates between a traveler and his or her surroundings.[12] The physical center moves out from the body and enters the strange new landscape. My approach seeks to reassign corporeality to the symbolic hearts in this text so that their full range of meaning in the contexts of this narrative might be fully appreciated. In his brief article, Greenblatt is speaking of a much less traumatic estrangement than the theft and consumption of a lover's heart or body, the forcible transplantation of a foreign heart into a sleeping woman's chest, or a widowed Trojan woman into Greek society. His definitions of the temporary strangeness of new surroundings and its effect on subjectivity, however, are also applicable to the traumatic estrangements in this text:

> Travel's estrangement-effect makes the external world not only more noticeable but more intense, just as poetry makes language more intense. The consequence is that the ratio of the self to everything that lies beyond the self changes: for a moment the world insists upon its own independent existence, its thingness apart from ourselves, and we are temporarily liberated from our own personal obsessions.[13]

Since the heart serves as the center of the essential functions of the body, the "thingness" of the heart estranged from itself makes the body more noticeable and more intense.[14] It also, I argue, renders the heart distinct from the body, making either it or the body from which it has departed a part of the landscape

---

12 Stephen Greenblatt, "Expectations and Estrangement," *The Threepenny Review* 67 (Autumn, 1996): 25–26.

13 Ibid., 25.

14 Bill Brown, "Thing Theory," *Critical Inquiry* 28, no. 1 (Autumn, 2001): 1–22. Brown explores the inescapability of things, including the body, as well as their capacity to interrupt the intentional processes of subject and object. Disconnecting the heart from the rest of the body's systems — "circuits of production and distribution" — draws our attention to its status as an object and gets in the way of our recognition of it as part of a whole.

rather than, or in addition to, the self. In both of these narratives, either the body or the heart, in Bill Brown's terms, "insists on its own independent existence," which makes its functions much more visible in relation to its human host(s). In this sense, the traveling body parts become, like the bridges in Sarah Breckenridge Wright's essay, the architectural manifestation of movement — they are vectors for elements of the self.

Given the *Middle English Dictionary* definition of "herte," the disorientation caused by these disincorporations of the heart is significant. The physical heart can refer to the organ itself or to the entire area around the heart, including the stomach, and is the seat of the soul and memory.[15] The MED states that the heart is symbolic of "the conscious self, the true self as opposed to the outward *persona,* the center of psychic and sensitive functions." Removing the heart from the body, then, decenters "the true self," and sorting out the pieces of the selves becomes particularly tricky when the heart is incorporated into a foreign body. These extractions should not be read as surgical procedures, however. Language of fear and aggression punctuates the removal of the heart. Maggie Kilgour uses the term *concordia discors* to describe a meeting of extremes, "although not in an equal relation but in an identity achieved through the subordination, even annihilation, of one of the terms." This explanation is especially applicable to the hearts' patterns of movement and damage.[16] Both words contain the root word for heart, one connoting unity, the other distance and separation. Likewise, in *Troilus and Criseyde,* what is external to the body is in constant, often violent, contact with what is internal. The subsequent "estrangement-effect" of the disembodied hearts enhances the reflective function of the text because it objectifies and renders foreign the organ most central to medieval notions of identity.

---

15 *Middle English Dictionary* online, s.v. "herte."
16 For a brief explanation of *concordia discors* in the context of cannibalistic power relations, see Maggie Kilgour, *From Communion to Cannibalism* (Princeton: Princeton University Press, 1990), 3.

## Foreign Territory

*Troilus and Criseyde* is a retelling of Boccacio's *Il Filostrato,* an early fourteenth-century tale about a romance between Troilus and Criseyde during the Trojan War. In the course of the poem, Troilus falls in love with the widow Criseyde, who considers herself unable to love, regardless of the suitor. After a dream in which an eagle steals her heart and transplants its own into her chest, Criseyde begins to warm up to Troilus. As I explained, Criseyde's uncle, Pandarus, acts as the mediator between the two lovers, so the locus of control is external to the lovers. Pandarus's impassioned speeches persuade Criseyde to fall in love with Troilus. As soon as she does, however, she is relocated to Greece against her will. The removal and objectification of the heart, here and elsewhere, emphasizes the external forces acting upon Criseyde, particularly upon her allegiances. Even Troilus's health becomes a source of external pressure, although it is clearly not the only deciding factor. Troilus begs Criseyde to remain faithful to him, but Criseyde symbolically transfers her allegiance to Diomede shortly after her arrival in Greece by pinning the ruby brooch on him.

In keeping with this cultural upheaval, the locus of control in *Troilus and Criseyde* is variable and complex. Pandarus tries to maintain control over the lovers through smooth-tongued manipulation. Troilus tries to keep Criseyde in check by pleading and bargaining, and Calchas and Diomede exercise political power and physical strength, respectively.[17] The exception, the one character who asserts power by replacing an internal structure of the body, is the eagle. He comes to Criseyde in a dream, and the violation is described in threatening terms:

---

[17] Robert Hanning calls Chaucer's Criseyde a "female 'text'" on which men — Troilus, Pandarus, the narrator — impose meanings that accord with their desires." See "Come in Out of the Code: Interpreting the Discourse of Desire in Boccaccio's *Filostrato* and Chaucer's *Troilus and Criseyde,*" in *Chaucer's* Troilus and Criseyde: *"Subgit to Alle Poesye" Essays in Criticism,* eds. R.A. Shoaf and Catherine S. Cox, 120–37 (Binghamton: Medieval & Renaissance Texts & Studies, 1992), 120.

> And as she slep, anonright tho hire mette
> How that an egle, fethered whit as bon,
> Under hir brest his longe clawes sette,
> And out hir herte he rente, and that anon,
> And dide his herte into hire brest to gon —
> Of which she not agroos, ne nothyng smerte —
> And forth he fleigh, with herte left for herte. (II:925–932)

The passage emphasizes his long claws and the language, in contrast with the reassurance in the last line that Criseyde does not feel any pain or fear, is violent and abrupt. Criseyde is evidently mercifully asleep, but the eagle has "seized" and "rent" her heart from her breast before putting his own in its place.

*Troilus and Criseyde* is predominately concerned with foreignness, and in particular foreign objects being introduced to bodies. Criseyde's new heart is the eagle's heart. While it appears that Criseyde's affections are altered by the eagle's heart since she begins to have feelings for Troilus after her heart is exchanged, that effect is ultimately temporary, since she symbolically replaces Troilus with Diomede. I would go so far as to say that the eagle's heart, and its attendant affections for Troilus, are always foreign to Criseyde, and that she might be imagined as embodying a perpetual state of disincorporation, consistently rejecting the transplant, which retains its object status because her body never incorporates it. Criseyde is, in a sense, a tourist by Greenblatt's definition: estrangement-effect centers on the temporary disorientation of the self within an unfamiliar physical environment. With regard to Criseyde's exchange of hearts in the poem, the agent of disorientation is fundamentally external. After she is exchanged for Antenor, her disorientation is compounded. Finally, by pinning her heart brooch on Diomede, she recovers some sense of orientation, expressing her loyalty to Greece, but also her rejection of Troilus:

> And after this the storie telleth us
> That she him yaf the faire baye stede
> The which he ones wan of Troilus;

> And eke a broche — and that was litel nede —
> That Troilus was, she yaf this Diomede.
> And ek, she bet from sorwe hym to releve
> She made hym were a pencel of hire sleve. (V:1037–1043)

This stanza makes clear that, not only did Criseyde give Diomede Troilus's possessions, but that it was unnecessary for her to do this. Here again, the framing of the narrative indicates that Criseyde's actions connote rejection or temporariness rather than full incorporation. In short, I propose that Criseyde experiences estrangement-effects imposed by others, but she also estranges herself from her heart and her environment in the poem — as evidenced by the simultaneously romantic and political act of pinning the brooch on Diomede. It is possible to see Greenblatt's concept at play in the ways in which Criseyde reacts to changes in her psyche as well as in her environment. The encounter itself is a violation of Criseyde, as Aranye Fradenburg notes, calling the eagle's theft "a simultaneous evocation and denial of violence, an image at once of overwhelming invasive power and of apparent reciprocity."[18] In much the same way that Criseyde acquiesces to being traded by her father, she appears to consent to participation in this exchange of hearts as well. Criseyde is involved in incorporation as a form of exchange, but the circumstances surrounding the event and the language used to describe it reinforce the idea that Criseyde is only a tourist.

### Foreign Exchange

After Criseyde's center has been replaced with a foreign object, and in the passages following the eagle's invasion, she is given no voice with which to protest in the passages following the eagle's invasion as the narrator moves on to concern himself with Troilus's return from "the scarmuch" while Criseyde sleeps (II:934).

---

18 Louise O. Fradenburg, "'Our owne wo to drynke': Loss, Gender, and Chivalry in Troilus and Criseyde," in *Chaucer's* Troilus and Criseyde, eds. Shoaf and Cox, 88–106, at, 99.

In effect, Criseyde is temporarily disabled and ignored. Her role is ostensibly passive. This effect is reinforced by her behavior toward Troilus. When Criseyde sees him again, her heart responds differently to him:

> And how so she hath ben here-byforn,
> To God hope I, she hath now kaught a thorn,
> She shal nat pulle it out this nexte wyke.
> God sende mo swich thornes on to pike! (II:1271–1274)

The phrasing here indicates again, however, that the effect is temporary. Criseyde has "kaught a thorn," that she shall not pull out next week, but the thorn clearly will not remain in its place permanently, since the poet asks God to send more to pull out. Seeing that Criseyde is responding to Troilus's appearance, Pandarus begins to behave like the nightingale, stoking the fires of affection to keep Criseyde's new heart warm (I:1275–1282). The external forces surrounding Criseyde here take care to ensure that the carefully orchestrated transplant will be effective, and Pandarus appears to be trying to reinforce the link between the physiology of Criseyde's new heart and her affections, using his heart to stimulate hers: "I pray yow hertely."[19] The characterization of the thorns as temporary and subject to Criseyde's will, however, indicates that Pandarus's efforts are ultimately futile. The bodily damage Criseyde sustains in the eagle attack is not insignificant, but the text appears insistent that the wounds will heal and Criseyde will find a way to remove the thorns' influence.

This theme of distance is also reflected in the poem's frequent descriptions of hearts, which are most often stripped of their "stuffness."[20] The hearts that do take material form are objectified, and thereby removed from their function as bodily organs. Clark and Wasserman characterize those references in spatial

---

19 *Oxford English Dictionary Online*, s.v. "heartily, adv."
20 Ruth Evans, "When a Body Meets a Body: Fergus and Mary in the York Cycle," *New Medieval Literatures* 1 (1997): 193–212, at 194.

terms, saying that the heart was either framed as a vessel or a thing to be placed in a vessel, like the heart in the body. They go on to argue that the symbolic functions of the heart merge in the exchanges of hearts in the poem.[21] The ruby brooch contains a stone in the shape of a heart and the structure of exchange renders it "real" in much the same way as any currency becomes real — through the ritual of transaction. Once Criseyde reaches Greece, she — after a brief moment of inner conflict — transfers her allegiance to Diomede, pinning the ruby brooch, an objectified heart, that Troilus had given her, onto his collar. The heart brooch as a symbol has such a profound effect on Troilus because it can be lost, and its absence is tangible in terms of weight, temperature, etc., in addition to its sentimental and symbolic value. Similarly, even in the context of a dream, the eagle's heart is given shape and heft. His claws tear open Criseyde's body and invade it. Subsequent emotional changes occur *in addition* to the material alterations of the body, and the effects of the transplant that extend outside of the dreamscape into Criseyde's waking life substantiate the link between the dream and Criseyde's reality.

In accordance with the tradition of the *stilnovisti*, Troilus assigns blame to Criseyde for his troubles rather than blaming the God of Love for shooting him and thus setting off this torturous chain of events. As we find out shortly hereafter, Criseyde gifts her heart to Troilus:

> Soone after this they spake of sondry thynges,
> As fel to purpos of this aventure,
> And pleyinge entrechaungeden hire rynges,
> Of whiche I kan nought tellen no scripture;
> But wel I woot, a broche, gold and asure,
> In which a ruby set was lik an herte,
> Criseyde hym yaf, and stak it on his sherte. (III:1366–1371)

---

21 Clark and Wasserman, "The Heart in *Troilus and Criseyde*.

In this scene, Criseyde has the power over the movement of the symbolic heart. In the same way that the eagle was previously able to remove its own heart, Criseyde is now transplanting a heart, and the language of "sticking" in which the act is couched recalls the thorn that Criseyde had previously "caught" and the eagle's claws that deposited it. We might read this as Criseyde's gentle distancing of her heart from herself, although this does not negate the exchange as a gesture of love and loyalty. It does, however, render the heart more external and portable, and make it easier to understand how Criseyde feels free to transfer it to Diomede. Clark and Wasserman have argued that Chaucer makes clear in this scene that the brooch is not Criseyde's heart, but the structure of the lines do not specify where the uncertainty lies: "Men seyn, I not, that she yaf him hir herte" (v:1050). I argue that the eagle's transplant could just as easily be the source of the uncertainty. Criseyde may be giving Diomede the heart she has — it is just not hers. If this is the case, and the heart was never truly hers, re-gifting it to Diomede is less of an act of treachery than if she were giving the center of herself to him. Criseyde's objectified hearts are notably malleable in some way, which indicates that she is affected by external forces and subject to affections. They are, however, unusually distant, portable, and foreign, which suggests that her affections are similarly distant, portable, and foreign to her. This does not mean that she is cold or heartless, but that the heat and proximity of her heart have largely been manipulated by external forces, until she learns to manipulate them in similar ways herself.

### Criseyde's Slippery Heart: Misdirection and Disorientation

Criseyde's "slydynge of corage" is often discussed as her heart's movement, but the challenge throughout the poem appears to be that her suitors have difficulty clinging to it.[22] Even the nar-

---

22 *Slydynge* can mean unstable or deceitful, but it can also mean elusive. See MED online, s.v. "slidinge, ppl." For alternate readings, see Frieda Elaine Penninger, *Chaucer's* Troilus and Criseyde *and* The Knight's Tale (Lanham:

rator has difficulty reconciling her physical appearance with her age (v:826). As Sheila Delany has observed, the portraits of the characters are oddly located near the end of the poem, which she identifies as an alienating function — one of many she examines.[23] Criseyde and her heart are also frequently distanced from each other toward the end of the poem, but she seems to make attempts to control the heart's movement. She calls herself lost, but says her heart is true, which indicates a separation of her heart from her self. She even sets her heart on fire in remembrance of Troilus's words, which is a divine office in Dante's *Vita nuova*. Both Troy and Troilus slip through her heart in Book V, but this is attributed to their inability to stick rather than hers:

'For which, with-outen any wordes mo,
To Troye I wol, as for conclusioun.'
But god it wot, er fully monthes two,
She was ful fer fro that entencioun.
For bothe Troilus and Troye toun
Shal knotteles through-out hir herte slyde;
For she wol take a purpos for tabyde. (v:764–770)

While Criseyde remains fixed, both Troy and Troilus slip knotless through her heart, which is clearly cast here as a vessel. In the next stanza, Diomede resorts to a hook and line in his attempt to anchor himself to her slippery heart, and a few stanzas later, he again entreats her to let Troy and Troilus pass through her heart (v:911–917).[24]

In closing, I will examine this fixedness of Criseyde's heart as a function of its objectified form. Criseyde's declaration that her heart is "faste" on Troilus appears to indicate that she is faithful

---

University Press of America, 1993), 71; Florence H. Ridley, "A Plea for the Middle Scots," in *The Learned and the Lewed: Studies in Chaucer and Medieval Literature,* eds. Larry Dean Benson and Bartlett Jere Whiting (Cambridge: Harvard University Press, 1974), 175–96.

23 Sheila Delaney, "Techniques of Alienation in *Troilus and Criseyde,*" in *Chaucer's* Troilus and Criseyde, eds. Shoaf and Cox, 29–46.

24 *MED* online, s.v. "passen."

to him, but the poem repeatedly resists these simple readings. Given the function of the brooch throughout the narrative, I want to explore an alternate reading: that "faste" indicates physical fastening rather than committed love. Read this way, the stanza mirrors the way Criseyde "caught a thorn" as a result of the eagle exchanging its heart for hers:

> As she that hadde hir herte on Troilus
> So faste, that ther may it noon arace;
> And straungely she spak, and seyde thus;
> 'O Diomede, I love that ilke place
> Ther I was born; and Ioves, for his grace,
> Delivere it sone of al that doth it care!
> God, for thy might, so leve it wel to fare! (v:953–959)

This reading gives Criseyde credit for her good intentions — she fastened her heart on Troilus so that no one could take it out, but her heart is slippery. Her real love, as she states shortly after, remains with her dead husband (v:974–980). It is also noteworthy that she spoke "straungely," which indicates either unusual speech or foreign or wild language.[25] In her response to Troilus's subsequent impassioned pleas for her healing presence, Criseyde states that she has no heart or health to send (v:1590–1596). Following the movement of the brooch, this could be because she has gifted it to Diomede.

If this is the case, the symbol of the brooch works on many levels, since the word in Middle English could mean either an ornament or a weapon.[26] In the midst of a lengthy discussion of the brooch in Book V, just after Troilus finds the brooch on Diomede's collar, he accuses Criseyde's heart of slaying him:

> 'Who shal now trowe on any othes mo?
> Allas, I never wolde han wend, er this,
> That ye, Criseyde, coude han chaunged so;

---

25 *MED* online, s.v. "straungeli."
26 *MED* online, s.v. "broche."

> Ne, but I hadde a-gilt and doon amis,
> So cruel wende I not your herte, y-wis,
> To slee me thus; allas, your name of trouthe
> Is now for-doon, and that is al my routhe. (v:1681–1687)

The juxtaposition of Criseyde's slippery heart and everyone's attempts to find a way to affix it or affix themselves to it seem to emphasize the dual function of Criseyde's slippery heart as vessel and a thing to be placed in a vessel. This brings us to the final relevant definition of "broche," which is to pierce a container, letting the contents flow out. Emphasizing the fragility and vulnerability of the human body, this cluster of connotations reminds readers that, as Christopher Roman has noted, "[T]he body is porous, mediated by elements, implicated with matter." In the following stanza, Troilus uses the word *feffe*, a word heavy with both territorial and financial connotations:

> 'Was ther non other broche yow liste lete
> To feffe with your newe love,' quod he,
> 'But thilke broche that I, with teres wete,
> Yow yaf, as for a remembraunce of me?
> Non other cause, allas, ne hadde ye
> But for despyt, and eek for that ye mente
> Al-outrely to shewen your entente! (v:1688–1694)

The narrator ends by enjoining readers to "cast all our hearts on heaven," contrasting God's love with the counterfeit loves in the poem. The theoretical payoff from examining this kind of bodily estrangement in medieval narratives is that it highlights the tension between the identification and abjection inherent in the relationship between bodies and travel. Travel is always an exercise in taking in what is desirable and affirming, while at once keeping out what is threatening and destabilizing. In the case of Criseyde, foreignness is initially introduced from outside influences, but as a result of the many transplants she undergoes in the narrative, she begins to embody foreignness by the end of the narrative.

## Conclusion

Historical theologian Barbara Newman has explored the implications of heart transplants and exchanges in medieval literature through both theological and medical lenses. Observing the unifying capacity of Christ's sacrifice in mystical hagiography, Newman contrasts the exchange of hearts with Christ in medieval literature with exchanges between humans.[27] Whether spiritual or medical, however, she acknowledges that exchanges of hearts are often characterized by "alarming literalism."[28] Observing this intrusion of a foreign organ so often described in medieval literature in graphic and violent terms, Newman echoes Jean-Luc Nancy in her description of heart transplant as a "long process of self-alienation, induced by the medically altered body."[29] This process of self-alienation, I argue, overlaps in theoretically significant ways with the process of self-alienation threatened by medieval travel.

Returning to Verdon's description of territory, exchange, and movement as the three physical realities of medieval travel, it is clear that the ontological threats posed by travel and heart transplant are functionally similar. Nancy refers to the transplanted heart as "the intruder" who does not lose his strangeness, and insists that as long as he remains foreign, "his coming will not cease."[30] This frames the body as the territory upon which the foreign heart intrudes, and which is characterized by openness and violability. The exchange of hearts is accompanied by a loss of subjectivity, and that loss is compounded by the battle to keep one's own body from rejecting the foreign heart:

---

[27] Barbara Newman, "*Iam cor meum non sit tuum*: Exchanging Hearts, from Heloise to Helfta," *From Knowledge to Beatitude: St. Victor, Twelfth-Century Scholars, and Beyond* (Notre Dame: University of Notre Dame Press, 2013), 281–99.

[28] Barbara Newman, "Exchanging Hearts: A Medievalist Looks at Transplant Surgery," *Rethinking the Medieval Legacy for Contemporary Theology* (Notre Dame: University of Notre Dame Press, 2014), 17–41.

[29] Ibid., 20.

[30] Jean-Luc Nancy, "L'Intrus," *CR: The New Centennial Review* 2, no. 3 (2002): 1–14, at 2.

"As soon as intrusion occurs, it multiplies, making itself known through its continually renewed internal differences." The result, says Nancy, is disorientation: "One emerges from this adventure lost." These structural similarities between travel and transplant have remained remarkably consistent from their representation in medieval literature to their psychological and cultural ramifications in the twenty-first century. This structural consistency may offer insight into modern medical and psychopharmaceutical conversations as much as it gives us greater insight into the intricate interplay between matter, affect, and movement in the Middle Ages.

3

# *Whan I schal passyn hens*
## Moving With/In *The Book of Margery Kempe*

*Robert Stanton*

### A Protean Text: The Invention of Margery Kempe

*The Book of Margery Kempe,* dating from the late 1430s, bristles with concurrent transits, passages, and thoroughfares in all sorts of modes, scales, and palettes. Most obviously, the book's shifting, shifty generic status incessantly confronts the reader's expectations, demands, and avenues of understanding. Unequal parts autobiography, confessional, saintly résumé, pilgrimage narrative, devotional program, and psychodrama, the text continuously provokes its medieval and modern users to ask what it *is* and what it is *for*.

Almost any scene, whether a conversation with Jesus, a confrontation with a powerful churchman, or an anecdote about the travails of pilgrimage, can seem to serve the exemplary program of one genre then, with a shriek, drop into place in another story altogether. Such discontinuities of expectation and reception are further complicated by the volatile, rapidly developing narrator, Margery, or Kempe, or Margery Kempe, who rarely if ever reveals a fully traceable narrative sequence, an inarguable didactic goal, or a wholly comprehensible psychological or emotional state.¹ Then there is the constant question of Kempe's level of control: of her own psychological and emotional state, of the people and institutions who support or persecute her — and especially of the text itself, which may be the result of a collaboration with at least two probably male scribes.²

These large questions about the status, function, and value of *The Book of Margery Kempe* remain intense objects of debate in the burgeoning body of scholarship and criticism on the topic. In this essay, I want to address several specific modes of transit within and around the *Book*. First, I examine the physical sites that generated and maintained Kempe's geographical and

---

1 Lynn Staley, in *Margery Kempe's Dissenting Fictions* (University Park: Penn State University Press, 1994), distinguishes the book's author, "Kempe" from its subject, "Margery." Although I am not as confident as Staley about the presence of an authoritative, controlling author, Staley's productive distinction has reset the conversation about the authorial presence in the text. While this question remains open, however, I use "Kempe" here in order to avoid the double standard of referring to male authors ("Chaucer") and female authors ("Margery").

2 On the scribal situation, see John C. Hirsh, "Author and Scribe in *The Book of Margery Kempe*," *Medium Ævum* 44 (1975): 145–50; Staley, *Margery Kempe's Dissenting Fictions*, ch. 1; Nicholas Watson, "The Making of *The Book of Margery Kempe*," in *Voices in Dialogue: Reading Women in the Middle Ages*, eds. Linda Olson and Kathryn Kerby-Fulton, 395–434 (Notre Dame: University of Notre Dame Press, 2005). On the authorial voice, see Karma Lochrie, *Margery Kempe and Translations of the Flesh* (Philadelphia: University of Pennsylvania Press, 1991); Sarah Beckwith, "Problems of Authority in Late Medieval English Mysticism: Language, Agency, and Authority in *The Book of Margery Kempe*," *Exemplaria* 4 (1992): 172–99; David Lawton, "Voice, Authority, and Blasphemy in *The Book of Margery Kempe*," in *Margery Kempe: A Book of Essays*, ed. Sandra J. McEntire, 93–115 (New York: Garland, 1992); Diane R. Uhlman, "The Comfort of Voice, the Solace of Script: Orality and Literacy in *The Book of Margery Kempe*," *Studies in Philology* 91 (1994): 50–69; Liz Herbert McAvoy, *Authority and the Female Body in the Writings of Julian of Norwich and Margery Kempe* (Woodbridge and Rochester: D.S. Brewer, 2004); Felicity Riddy, "Text and Self in *The Book of Margery Kempe*," in *Voices in Dialogue*, 435–53; Albrecht Classen, "Margery Kempe as Writer: A Woman's Voice in the Mystical and Literary Discourse," in *The Power of a Woman's Voice in Medieval and Early Modern Literatures*, 271–308 (Berlin: Walter de Gruyter, 2007); and Joel Fredell, "Design and Authorship in *The Book of Margery Kempe*," *Journal of the Early Book Society* 12 (2009): 1–28.

spiritual development, and the motion between those sites that conditioned the nature and effects of that development. The narrative privileges Kempe's frequent journeys within England and throughout Europe and the Holy Land, which function not only as narrative arcs but also as a stimulating medium for some paired movements within Kempe's experiential world: spiritual transformation and social development, the simultaneous enactment and manipulation of devotional programs, the active and contemplative lives, and the negotiation between the book's putative exemplary agenda and Kempe's particular psychological and emotional landscape. Second, I examine the relationship between Kempe's inner and outer devotional narratives, and the ways in which she consciously or unconsciously manipulates them in the service of a new spiritual paradigm. Third, I situate the book's geographical and structural shifts within two networks of people and institutions, one supporting and advancing Kempe, one persecuting and hindering her, but both of them creating and defining her, with and without her participation. Finally, I move from the thoroughfares within the Book itself to several modes of transit outside the work that both reflect and condition the internal passages; namely, the shifting critical characterization of "Margery Kempe" as both author and subject of the book, and the pedagogical trends that are helping new generations of students negotiate the troubled issues of voice and authority raised by the text.

### Spiritual Cartography: Margery Maps Christendom

From her home base in Lynn, Kempe visits numerous places in Norfolk and the neighboring counties of Lincolnshire and Cambridgeshire, moving west to Leicestershire, Gloucestershire, and Bristol, as far north as Yorkshire, and south to London and Kent, visiting towns, churches, abbeys, episcopal sees, and port cities on her way abroad to Norway, Poland, Germany, the Netherlands, France, Spain, Italy, and the Holy Land. The book configures stasis and movement as interdependent modes: Kempe's mystical experiences, including her conversations with God and Jesus, tend to happen while she is located in a single place, whether in a church while praying or hearing a sermon, in her own house, at designated pilgrimage sites, or at a way station during her travels. But the movement between those places creates the conditions for those experiences. She loves to hear the word of God preached, so she must travel to where a sermon is being delivered; pilgrimage by its nature involves physical travel to approved pilgrimage sites, where she goes well beyond the recommended degree of affective engagement to cultivate her ongoing relationship with God; and she frequently visits clerics and holy men and women in search of approval and support. Such interdependence between enabling travel and place-based spiritual experience reflects a broader dynamic between place and motion: as both Schneider and Van Dyke note in this volume, the concept of place, as well as the function of individual places in economic and cultural systems, is dependent on the ability and phenomenon of moving between those places.

Thus, Kempe's motion is continual rather than continuous: her devotional exercises, ecstasies, torments, and conversations with Christ take places in moments of relative physical stasis, notwithstanding the writhing and wallowing she performs, which I do not characterize as transit. Her spiritual journeying, though, cannot begin until she comes through the dramatically obstructive crisis that begins the book. Kempe is mentally and physically immobilized before and after the birth of her first child: by illness during pregnancy, by her labor and her fear of death, by her confessor's failure to listen and give counsel, by her subsequent torment by demonic visions, and finally by being literally bound, "that sche mygth not have hir wylle [...] that men wend sche schuld nevyr a skapyd ne levyd."[3] Kempe is bound, stuck, and stopped in every possible way: only when Jesus visits her for the first time can she break free of her physical and psychological bonds and begin the incessant physical and spiritual

---

3   All quotations are from *The Book of Margery Kempe*, ed. Lynn Staley (Kalamazoo: Medieval Institute Publications, 1996), 1.1.165–66. Citations are by book, chapter, and line number.

transit that frames her spiritual life. Kempe's constant physical displacement during her travels around England and Europe crucially constitute her ongoing self-fashioning, both generating and revealing an unstable identity. The book's stated purpose ("a schort tretys and a comfortabyl for synful wrecchys, wherin thei may have gret solas and comfort to hem and undyrstondyn the hy and unspecabyl mercy of ower sovereyn Savyowr Cryst Jhesu," 1.introduction.1.) conditions, but fails to contain, her incomplete, experimental, and endlessly renewed self-creation.

Tracing the occurrences of the richly polysemous Middle English verb "passen" in the text reveals layers of spatial, temporal, metaphoric, and affective movement, of people, events, and natural and mystical phenomena. The word occurs thirty-five times in the *Book,* yielding a beautiful variety of passings: Margery and John Kempe passing forth in their journeyings, Margery desiring chastisement and rebuke because "Alle hys apostlys, martyres, confessorys, and virgynes and alle that evyr comyn to hevyn passed be the wey of tribulacyon" (1.3.287–88), and the passing forth, passing by, and passing away of the sounds, smells, and images that sustain her. "Passen" occurs in a spatial sense only thirteen times, most of the travel being expressed with forms of "come" or "go." Of the non-spatial occurrences, only five are temporal; the remaining seventeen usages – half of the total – concern mystical transcendence, experience, endurance, or death. The sounds and melodies Kempe hears in her contemplation "passyd hir witte for to tellyn hem" (1.89.5214–15) she "passyd many perellys" (2.5.301–2) in her dangerous travels in Book Two, and she expresses her own hopes and Christ's promises about what will transpire at the end of earthly life, as she takes leave of her confessor in Rome, trusting to meet again "in her kendly cuntré whan thei wer passyd this wretchyd wordelys exile" (1.2358–59 ). In fact, fully eight occurrences of "passen," often with an added phrase such as "owt of this world," signify death, usually Kempe's, as she anticipates union with God in the next world. As we shall see, the metaphorical, transcendent, and eschatological passings in the book are mapped onto, and expressed, by the physical journeys Kempe undertakes.

Kempe's travels incorporate many of the most popular pilgrimage sites of the late Middle Ages: Hailes Abbey in Gloucestershire (said to house a vial of Christ's blood), the Brigittine monastery of Mt Sion in Shene, Wilsnack and Aachen in Germany, and the "big three" of Santiago de Compostela in Spain, Rome, and Jerusalem and its environs. At these holy places, she continues the crying that she habitually practiced closer to home, notably her own church of St. Margaret's in Lynn. On Mt. Calvary, she "fel down that sche mygth not stondyn ne knelyn but walwyd and wrestyd wyth hir body, spredyng hir armys abrode, and cryed wyth a lowde voys as thow hir hert schulde a brostyn asundyr," which the book's narrator says was "the fyrst cry that evyr sche cryed in any contemplacyon," carefully distinguishing it from her previous "wepyng," which was brought on by various stimuli including her own sins, those of others, and the thought of Christ's passion.

Although the pilgrimage sites, especially Santiago, Rome, and Jerusalem, were approved and encouraged as spiritual destinations, among Kempe's trips inside and outside England there is a high degree of continuity between pilgrimage strictly defined and her journeys to seek support and advice. As David Wallace has noted, Kempe never appears homesick or closely identified with England while she is abroad. While in Norway on Easter Sunday, she views the raising of a cross and "had hir meditacyon and hir devocyon wyth wepyng and sobbyng as wel as yf sche had ben at hom" (2.3.246–47).[4] The passage locates the most accustomed site of her weeping as "home," whether this means Lynn or England, and establishes her devotional weeping as the same thing wherever it occurs. The relationship between Margery's position at home and her identity as a frequent pilgrim evinces the tension between a penitential self as an acting

---

4  David Wallace, "Periodizing Women: Mary Ward (1585–1645) and the Premodern Canon," *Journal of Medieval and Early Modern Studies* 36 (2006): 397–453, at 412.

subject and an apophatic, negated self that participates in a macrocosmic community of penitential pilgrims (Roman, in this volume, discusses this double penitential identity in terms of the Foucauldian concept of the self realizing itself in a spiritual context). Kempe, however, is a limit case for this inside/outside movement: the idiosyncrasies of her highly personal and individual relationship with Jesus constantly limit her full participation in the structured, institutional practices of devotional life.

Kempe also travels frequently to see people from whom she needs advice, official support, verification of her pious practices, or simply spiritual companionship. Examples include the Archbishops of Canterbury and York, the Norwich vicar Richard Caister, the Carmelite friar Alan of Lynn, and the anchoress Julian of Norwich. These trips share some characteristics with her pilgrimages proper: she is often told by God to visit a particular person, she frequently experiences hardships along the way, and her ultimate goal is to perform and demonstrate her own piety, whether in a Christian fellowship or as a figure of excess, disruption, and perceived heterodoxy. Sometimes her devotional practices even wear off on others, as when Thomas Marchale of Newcastle wept tears of contrition and compunction at Kempe's example (1.45.2536–42). Kempe's journeys have not one destination but many: each stop is a further stage of her self-creation and self-protection, and the trips themselves constitute a web of self-signification. But her pilgrimages, strictly defined, raise the stakes of this process: her enactment of the *vita Christi* and her apostolic tendencies can begin in England, but can only be fully developed in the Holy Land.

### Inside of the Outside: Margery, Kempe, and the World

The inner and outer journeys Kempe undertakes throughout the book mutually constitute one another, providing one of the most consistent and coherent structural patterns in a text known for its gaps, discontinuities, and lack of temporal unity. It is impossible to imagine Margery Kempe remaining in a single place for long, and if she did, she could not have created, developed, and nurtured her spiritual and emotional self. Conversely, her travels would not be so fraught, so laden with meaning, if she were less idiosyncratic and more in harmony with religious and political institutions and with other people. The book is in no way a traditional travel narrative: its subject is not the physical, practical aspects of traveling but Kempe's feelings and experiences, which are nonetheless inseparable from her relationships with people and places, whether helpful or obstructive.[5]

Nor is the enactment of an inner spiritual landscape by means of physical journeying an obvious one. Pilgrimage was enjoined on Christians as a spiritual duty, but the reality of travel, with its loosening of social bonds, its gender mixing, and its remaking of the public sphere led to fears that pilgrims sought worldly rather than spiritual rewards. Lollard critics like William Thorpe were especially hard on pilgrimage: most pilgrims, claimed Thorpe, "despise God and all His commandments and Saints."[6] From the early Middle Ages onward, large numbers of women went on pilgrimage, although it is significant that many of the early (fourth- and fifth-century) female saints who went on pilgrimage did so dressed as men.[7] The Crusades saw an increase in female pilgrimage, but throughout the high and late Middle Ages, nuns were strongly discouraged from the practice: Hildegard of Bingen strongly dissuaded a fellow abbess from a pilgrimage that she called "the devil's deceit."[8] The motives for

---

5 Staley, *Dissenting Fictions*, 190; Terence N. Bowers, "Margery Kempe as Traveler," *Studies in Philology* 97 (2000): 1–28, at 18–21; Ruth Summar McIntyre, "Margery's 'Mixed Life': Place Pilgrimage and the Problem of Genre in *The Book of Margery Kempe*," *English Studies* 89 (2008): 643–61, at 646–47.

6 *The Examination of Master William Thorpe*, in *Fifteenth Century Prose and Verse*, ed. Alfred W. Pollard (Westminster: Archibald Constable and Co., 1903), 140. Cited in Staley, *Dissenting Fictions*, 189–90.

7 Sylvia Schein, "Bridget of Sweden, Margery Kempe and Women's Jerusalem Pilgrimages in the Middle Ages," *Mediterranean Historical Review* 14 (1999): 44–58, at 45.

8 Hildegard of Bingen, *Epistolae*, PL 197: 329–30; trans. Peter Dronke, *Women Writers of the Middle Ages* (Cambridge: Cambridge University Press, 1984), 186–87. Cited in Schein, "Bridget of Sweden," 48.

Kempe's own pilgrimages were intensely personal and interior: her enactment of a highly communal Christian duty, culminating in the *imitatio Christi* in Jerusalem, was essential to her maintenance of her highly individual relationship with Jesus and her self-creation as a holy woman.

The canonical framing of the inner/outer distinction in pilgrimage terms was the dyad of the earthly and heavenly Jerusalems.[9] Seeking and visiting the heavenly Jerusalem was a deeply interior process, and the discouragement of nuns from making pilgrimages demonstrates that under the right conditions, the journeys to each Jerusalem were in fact separable: for monastics and nuns especially, only one Jerusalem needed to be sought: as Hildegard of Bingen put it, nuns are permanently "on their journey to the heavenly Jerusalem."[10] But Kempe's secular status, and her desire for an intensely physical, affective relationship with Christ, made her perhaps the most enthusiastic Jerusalem pilgrim ever. The moment she enters Jerusalem, she stresses the desire for the simultaneous achievement of the earthly and heavenly cities: "And, whan this creatur saw Jerusalem, rydyng on an asse, sche thankyd God wyth al hir hert, preyng hym for hys mercy that lych as he had browt hir to se this erdly cyté Jerusalem he wold grawntyn hir grace to se the blysful cité of Jerusalem abovyn, the cyté of hevyn" (1.28.1552–55 ). In so quickly conjoining the physical and spiritual places, Kempe hews closely to prescribed devotional pathways, as does her traversal, immediately following in the text, of the *via dolorosa* where Christ suffered his pains; at every stop, Kempe "wept and sobbyd so plentyuowsly as thow sche had seyn owyr Lord wyth hir bodyly ey sufferyng hys Passyon at that tyme" (1.28.1569–70)·

Nonetheless, the inner and outer aspects of Kempe's journeys were never perfectly coterminous and never led to a clear spir-

---

9  On pilgrimage generally and the two Jerusalems in particular, see Dee Dyas, *Pilgrimage in Medieval English Literature, 700–1500* (Cambridge: D.S. Brewer, 2001).

10  Hildegard of Bingen, *Scivias* 2.5.6; trans. Columba Hart and Jane Bishop, *Hildegard of Bingen: Scivias* (New York: Paulist Press, 1990). Cited in Schein, "Bridget of Sweden," 49.

itual resolution. Nicholas Watson notes that although Kempe seems like one of the "symple creatures" making up the imagined readership of *The Mirror of the Blessed Life of Christ* (Nicholas Love's early-fifteenth-century adaptation of the Pseudo-Bonaventure *Meditationes Vitae Christi*), and despite her eagerness to experience the earthly and heavenly Jerusalems together, she ignores "all the calls to ascend to contemplation of the heavenly city or God in his essence enunciated by texts like [Walter Hilton's] *The Scale of Perfection*."[11] Furthermore, as Terence Bowers has noted, by the standard of almost all pilgrimage narratives, the text's narration of Kempe's journey home is unusual: "Since the Jerusalem pilgrimage metaphorically enacts the journey of life, it ends in Jerusalem just as one's life should ideally end in the heavenly Jerusalem." As is the case with many places in the text that anchor Kempe firmly in the social world of creatures and institutions, her pilgrimage practices do not bring her fully into a heavenly world that transcends the earthly one. In fact, as pilgrimage became increasingly focused on saints and on well-worn prescribed routes in the later Middle Ages, it became much more difficult for it to serve a transformative spiritual function: as Dee Dyas puts it, "The rising profile of saints as intermediaries between a holy God and sinful human beings was paralleled by a danger that pilgrimage to an earthly goal could obscure or even undermine the longer-term goal of reaching the heavenly Jerusalem."[12]

Kempe's specific practices while on pilgrimage further complicate the relationship between her inner spiritual journey and her ongoing physical and social movements. At God's request, she wears white clothes, remaking herself as a virgin and incurring the wrath and scorn of her fellow-pilgrims. Most obviously, her continual weeping and writhing, even more abroad than in England, exposes her to harsh criticism from her fellow pilgrims. Hope Phyllis Weissman notes Kempe's close identification with the Virgin Mary's violent weeping on Calvary, as established in

---

11  Watson, "The Making," 416.
12  Dyas, *Pilgrimage,* 65.

the apocryphal *Gesta Pilati* and Robert Manning's paraphrase of the *Meditationes Vitae Christi*. Kempe's own behavior closely echoes those texts: "than sche fel down and cryed wyth lowde voys, wondyrfully turnyng and wrestyng hir body on every syde, spredyng hir armys abrode as yyf sche schulde a deyd, and not cowde kepyn hir fro crying" (1.28.1621–23).[13] Weissman goes further to claim that the phrase "wondyrfully turning and wrestyng" suggests the pain of labor; while not everyone will be convinced by the evidence of the passage alone, Weissman goes on to note that the first time Kempe weeps and writhes together is just after she has borne her last child, and Jesus tells her not to have any more, as if "her compassionate weeping is being conceived as an alternative, spiritual childbirth."[14]

Comparing Kempe's extravagant behavior to labor pains finds further confirmation in the reaction of Margery's male contemporary, the German Dominican friar Felix Fabri, to female weeping in Jerusalem: "Super omnes autem mulieres peregrinae sociae nostrae et sorores quasi parturientes clamabant, ullulabant et flebant." ("Above all, however, the female pilgrims, our companions and sisters, as if giving birth, cried out, wailed and wept.")[15] Kempe is consciously or unconsciously manipulating both devotional programs and contemporary expectations to perform a new kind of piety, modeled on existing modes but focused much more intensely on a performing individual. Some critics have seen in Margery Kempe a canny performance artist who turns herself, the devotional observer, into the subject of at-

---

13 Hope Phyllis Weissman, "Margery Kempe in Jerusalem: *Hysterica Compassio* in the Late Middle Ages," in *Acts of Interpretation: The Text and its Contexts 700–1600,* eds. Mary J. Carruthers and Elizabeth D. Kirk (Norman: Pilgrim Books, 1992), 209–15. See also Naöe Kukita Yoshikawa, "The Jerusalem Pilgrimage: The Centre of the Structure of *The Book of Margery Kempe*," *English Studies* 86 (2005): 193–2015, at 200.
14 Weissman, "Margery Kempe in Jerusalem," 212–13.
15 Fratris Felicis Fabri, *Evagatorum in Terrae Sanctae, Arabiae et Egypti Peregrinationem,* ed. Conrad D. Hassler (Stuttgart: Bibliothek des Literarischen Vereins, 2, 1843), 1.239 (my translation). Cited in Weissman, "Margery Kempe in Jerusalem," 215.

tention: she performs, as it were, the role of a pious holy woman, at home and abroad.[16]

## Exaltation and Revilement: Margery as Public Battlefield

Whatever degree of conscious performativity we want to attribute to Kempe, there is no doubt that she could not have achieved the effect she did without the participation of other people and institutions. All the book's movements need to be assessed, traced, and mapped on, around, and within the meaning-generating networks within the text. The most palpable network, and the one that gives the narrative much of its forward movement, is a human one organized around a dramatic opposition. On the one hand are Kempe's supporters, a community whose integrity (in the narrator's eyes) is strengthened not only by its geographical span but by the extended vertical social axis along which they range, from poor lay people in England and Europe through religious of all shapes and sizes and the merchant and gentry classes to aristocrats, bishops, and archbishops. We could visualize this community as an axis on a graph of economic, social, and religious importance; as a long cosmological line between the wicked earth and the joys of heaven; the mast of a tall ship bearing the heroine and her fellow-travelers on their sea-travels; or perhaps a prodigiously long pilgrim staff carried by Margery herself. These people construct her as a holy woman with access to the divine, support her physically and emotionally, and enable her movements in space.

---

16 For Kempe as performer, see Nanda Hopenwasser, "Margery Kempe as Comic Performer," *Magistra* 5 (1999): 69–77; Bowers, "Margery Kempe as Traveler," 2, 24–26; Susan Signe Morrison, *Women Pilgrims in Late Medieval England: Private Piety as Public Performance* (London and New York: Routledge, 2000), 128–41; Clare Bradford, "Mother, Maiden, Child: Gender as Performance in *The Book of Margery Kempe*," in *Feminist Poetics of the Sacred*, eds. Frances Devlin-Glass and Lyn McCredden (Oxford: Oxford Univerity Press, 2001), 165–81; Sheila Christie, "'Thei stodyn upon stolys for to beheldyn hir': Margery Kempe and the Power of Performance," *Studia Anglica Posnaniensia* 38 (2002): 93–103.

The matching and opposing human community consists of the antagonists who menace, harass, and damage Kempe in manifold ways: by threatening physical and sexual violence, by social ostracism, by spreading fear of her influence on other pious lay people, by accusing her of heresy, and by materially depriving her of food, clothing, and transport. This network bears almost the same social and religious range as the support network, although the very poor and the very powerful are less virulent than in the positive case; but in any case, the detractors also possess a vigor drawn from their geographical spread and social range, which is important for the discourse of revilement that crucially fuels Margery's spiritual identity. The two human networks are mutually sustaining, since veneration/appreciation and persecution/revilement are mutually constitutive, not only in a conceptual way but in the narrative's own terms (attention is repeatedly called to the contrast between supporters and detractors, and temporal shifts from one to the other are repeatedly highlighted as pivots in the drama).

The second network consists of stimuli, specifically physical sites and temporal occasions that both evoke and process Kempe's most acute spiritual responses, whether accompanied or not by the psychosomatic processes of crying, roaring, and wallowing. The physical sites include her home base of St Margaret's Church in Lynn, her own bedroom, open fields in the neighborhood, the abodes of holy people (Julian of Norwich, for example), and many pilgrimage sites, which themselves constitute a known, understood, and frequently negotiated social/religious network. The occasions include conversations with the deity (which are themselves in a dialogic relationship with events in her earthly life), listening to sermons, associational stimuli such as handsome men and boys, human and animal violence (all of which remind her of Jesus and his passion), and conscious participation in devotional exercises such as the *Meditationes Vitae Christi*.

All the significant crises and passings in the *Book* consist of relatively rapid transitions and transactions between the interdependent networks of support and revilement, as the narrative modulates between them within a chapter, a paragraph, or a sentence. The result is a main character always becoming and never being: as Margery ages and travels more frenetically in Book Two, even as she continues to nimbly negotiate the mutually reinforcing networks, her age raises the possibility of an endpoint preventing physical movement before her own death and apotheosis, a threat realized when she is forced to care for her injured and incapacitated husband. Both parts of the *Book* contain recognizable scapes and flows as defined by John Urry ("*Scapes* are the networks of machines, technologies, organizations, texts and actors that constitute various interconnected nodes along which *flows* can be relayed"), but their configurations are quite different. The much longer Book One features many episodes of contemplation and action underlying the incessant travel in England, Europe, and the Holy Land; the scapes, including the actors and institutions who defend and obstruct Kempe, are well-known and established entities by the start of Book Two, which is almost all travel. The main difference in the second book's scape is Kempe's age: she constantly fears for her own physical and sexual safety, clearly wonders whether she can continue to achieve the levels of bliss she wants, and at what cost, and longs ever more for death and transcendence.[17] In this respect, Kempe's travels reflect the key role, highlighted by Friedrich in this volume, of suffering and loss as constitutive properties of medieval travel. "Bodies," she notes, "are the primary territories in question"; Kempe's body functions as both the stakes of her spiritual venture (as she increasingly experiences physical danger and fear) and its reward (as her affective, physical relationship with Christ ripens into ever deeper identification).

---

17 John Urry, "Mobile Sociology," *British Journal of Sociology* 51 (2000): 185–203, at 193.

## All Roads Lead from Lynn: Margery, the Critics, and the Students

I want to conclude by moving from the thoroughfares within the *Book* itself to several modes of transit outside the work that relate to the internal passages. The first is critical, the second pedagogical. As the secondary work on Margery Kempe has grown on a steepening curve, critics and groups of critics have blazed paths that often intersect but all too frequently proceed in relative isolation from one another. But one clear dichotomy has emerged: between viewing Margery Kempe as a constructed late-medieval devotional subject and viewing her as an individual actor with a unique psyche and mental constructs not wholly explicable by existing discourses outside the *Book*. The pendulum has swung back and forth a couple of times now, from early works describing her as a "hysteric" to scholarly location of her within textual and devotional traditions to locating a female voice or discourse within a pattern of oppression to ever more insistent claims that she is a pattern, or close to a pattern, of a specific or general late-medieval devotional practice.

Reading recent work on Margery produces the impression of a pendulum oscillating ever more rapidly. Many recent studies apply to Margery's narrative moves adverbs such as "shrewdly," "cannily," and "astutely," risking an elision of her unique mental structures, including her sexual drives and traumatic reactions, while the fear of psychological explanation continues unabated; one recent study sternly warns against "pathologizing" Kempe and invokes the specter of American college students "donning the white coat," diagnosing her with ADHD, and prescribing Ritalin and Prozac; such warnings generally construct a straw-woman criticism in which any attempt to understand her individual mind is necessarily a project to isolate, silence, stifle, and dismiss her.[18] The best work, of course, grapples with

---

18 David Wallace, "Anchoritic Damsel: Margery Kempe of Lynn, c. 1373–c. 1440," *Strong Women: Life, Text, and Territory* 1347–1645 (Oxford: Oxford University Press, 2011), 79–80 and n. 51.

the combination of available discourse and individual mind; any understanding of the author and character based on one segment of that spectrum requires simultaneous awareness of, and negotiation with, the corresponding segment on the other side.[19] Institutional structures of knowledge and behavior (such as liturgy, devotional exercise, or pilgrimage) purporting to be stable, enforceable, and exemplified by Margery, are in fact occasions for self-created individual experience.

Pedagogically, the *Book* presents difficult problems of generic categorization, as it comprises elements of biography, perhaps autobiography, devotional treatise, and exemplum. Its generic instability is complicated by the range of options for teaching it. In a survey, probably via the excerpts in the *Norton Anthology of English Literature*, it falls implicitly within an English literary tradition; in a women's writing course, within a female tradition and raises contestable criteria such as "subversion" and "voice"; in a course on mystics, the very idea of a "tradition" risks imposing a stability that belies Margery's perpetual self-creation. Anyone teaching the *Book* needs to work with a virtual map, on which any locus opens up to multiple networks (narrative struc-

---

19 Scholarship on Kempe from 1934–2004 is usefully reviewed by Marea Mitchell, *The Book of Margery Kempe: Scholarship, Community, and Criticism* (New York: Peter Lang, 2005), 73–93; early works that explicitly pathologized Kempe in heavy-handed and ideologically driven ways are surveyed by Wallace, *Strong Women*, 75–79. Mary Hardiman Farley, "Her Own Creature: Religion, Feminist Criticism, and the Functional Eccentricity of Margery Kempe," *Exemplaria* 11 (1999): 1–21, is perhaps the most fully worked-out attempt to pathologize Margery Kempe. Unfortunately, the author is not a medieval scholar and takes no account of devotional paradigms or historical context. Raymond Powell, "Margery Kempe: An Exemplar of Late Medieval English Piety," *Catholic Historical Review* 89 (2003): 1–23, as its title implies, is perhaps the most extreme attempt to make Kempe an utterly normalized product of devotional discourse. M.K. Johnson, "'No Bananas, Giraffes, or Elephants': Margery Kempe's Text of Bliss," *Women's Studies* 21 (1992): 185–96 and Weissman, "Margery Kempe in Jerusalem" historicize hysteria, reveal its ideological underpinnings, and recuperate potentially progressive uses of the concept. Nancy Partner, "Reading The Book of Margery Kempe," *Exemplaria* 3 (1991): 29–66, remains the most balanced treatment, proposing a powerful combination of available religious discourse, psychological landscape, and literary composition.

tures, devotional programs, patterns of compulsion and repetition, transhistorical communities of holy women, and so on).

Digital humanities offers exciting possibilities for traversing the networks and thoroughfares within and around the *Book*. The *Mapping Margery Kempe* project at Holy Cross was a very early example of a digital medievalism, and though it has not been updated for some years, it remains a model of its kind, including a hyperlinked glossary of names, places, and concepts.[20] The manuscript of the Book has now been fully digitized and made available online through the British Library,[21] and Joel Fredell's *Book of Margery Kempe* project at Southeastern Louisiana University displays the digitized manuscript alongside a diplomatic transcription and promises a new reader's edition and interactive commentary by scholars and researchers.[22] David Wallace's project *Europe: A Literary History 1348–1418* is organized around "transnational sequences of interconnected places," and Gail McMurray Gibson and Theresa Coletti's segment "Norwich-Walshingham-Lynn" promises to incorporate Margery Kempe's movement within and outside England as an instance of textual, intellectual, and trade movements, including the heavily determined network of the Hanseatic League.[23] A similar editorial orientation could potentially do justice to the flows and scapes of the *Book of Margery Kempe* and its world, with important implications for pedagogy. The "flows" in the text are flows because they are both structured and dynamic, and the "scapes" are scapes because they are both perceivable in relation to other structures and negotiable by other actors. The beauty, and the utility, of the book lies in their interaction.

---

20 University of the Holy Cross, "Mapping Margery Kempe: A Guide to Late Medieval Material and Spiritual Life," last modified March 13, 2009, http://college.holycross.edu/projects/kempe/.

21 British Library, "Digitised Manuscripts: Add MS 61823," http://www.bl.uk/manuscripts/FullDisplay.aspx?ref=Add_MS_61823.

22 Southeastern Louisiana University, "The Book of Margery Kempe," http://english.selu.edu/humanitiesonline/kempe/index.php.

23 University of Pennsylvania, "Europe: A Literary History, 1348–1418: Norwich-Walshingham-Lynn," http://www.english.upenn.edu/~dwallace/europe/nodes/norwich.html.

4

# Animal Vehicles
# Mobility beyond Metaphor

*Carolynn Van Dyke*

In the book that inspired this one, John Urry redefines not just social structures but also the social agent. "[O]f course," he writes, "agents are not just humans but will be a variety of human and non-human actants that constitute the typical mobile, roaming hybrids."[1] Out of context, "non-human actants" would probably mean nonhuman animals; "roaming hybrids" might be peripatetic centaurs or cyborgs. In fact, however, the nonhuman actants that Urry discusses are principally objects, and his "hybrids" are "assemblages of humans, machines, and technologies."[2] Animals play only a passive role in his "mobile sociology," as the potential recipients of rights and "citizenship."[3]

Animals play a major role, however, in Urry's rhetoric. The last chapter of his *Sociology beyond Societies* centers on Zygmunt Bauman's contrast between two sociopolitical orders: "the gardening state," which "presumes exceptional concern with pattern, regularity and ordering, with what is growing and what should be weeded out;" and the "gamekeeper state," "concerned

---

1 John Urry, *Sociology beyond Societies: Mobilities for the Twenty-First Century* (New York: Routledge, 2000), 207.
2 Ibid., 4, 77–78.
3 Ibid., 169–72.

with regulating mobilities, with ensuring that there was sufficient stock for hunting in a particular site but not with the detailed cultivation of each animal in each particular place."[4] In Bauman's view, the former has replaced the latter: like gardeners, modern legislators and social scientists determine how to produce social order. In contrast, Urry sees a reversion to the gamekeeper model, in which "[a]nimals roamed around and beyond the estate, like the roaming hybrids that currently roam in and across national borders."[5] What interests me more than Urry's argument is the analogy that he deploys. Absent from the state's actual "roaming hybrids," animals serve as their metaphoric vehicle.

Urry makes clear in the second chapter of *Sociology beyond Societies*, titled "Metaphor," that he does not use figurative language carelessly, and his animal analogy is certainly apt. Nor is he unusual in referring to nonhuman animals only to clarify his sociological argument. Academic writing shares with imaginative literature and common speech the assumption that humans are fundamentally different from all other animals; any assertions of resemblance across that divide can only be metaphorical.[6] But classical and medieval thinkers might have regarded the vehicle of Urry's metaphor as singularly appropriate: to them, mobility defines animals. "In Latin," writes Isidore of Seville, "they are called animals (*animal*) or 'animate beings' (*animans*), because they are animated (*animare*) by life and moved

---

[4] Ibid., 188, 189; citing Zygmunt Bauman, *Legislators and Interpreters: On Modernity, Post-Modernity, and Intellectuals* (Ithaca: Cornell University Press, 1987).

[5] Urry, *Sociology beyond Societies*, 189.

[6] On humanity's ongoing attempts to establish this discontinuity, see, for instance, Giorgio Agamben, *The Open: Man and Animal* (Stanford: Stanford University Press, 2004), 12–16, 29, 38; Matthew Calarco, *Zoographies: The Question of the Animal from Heidegger to Derrida* (New York: Columbia University Press, 2008), 3; Jacques Derrida, "Eating Well, Or the Calculation of the Subject," in *Points...Interviews, 1974–1994*, trans. Peggy Kamuf, ed. Elisabeth Weber (Stanford: Stanford University Press, 1995), 89; and Roy G. Willis, *Signifying Animals* (London: Unwin Hyman, 1990), 7.

by spirit."⁷ John of Trevisa, translating Bartholomaeus Anglicus, writes that the "vertu [power] of moeuynge and of feelynge" is "in alle bestes," a category that includes "men and bestes wilde and tame."⁸ Similarly, at least one modern dictionary groups humans with other species on the basis of their common motility. According to the online *Merriam-Webster* dictionary an *animal* is simply a life form with "the capacity for spontaneous movement and rapid motor responses to stimulation." The definition goes on to distinguish the "lower animals" from "human beings" but cites no differentiae.⁹

In light of those definitions, mobility is the capacity that collapses the human tenor and animal vehicles of Urry's metaphors. In being provisioned for hunting but able to cross national boundaries, game animals are not *like* the human and institutional "hybrids" of the modern state; they are among those roaming agents. So too, the cultivated stock of a "gardening state" includes nonhuman animals (and hybrids). I propose, therefore, that we reformulate Urry's "mobile sociology" to include a fuller range of living actors. In this chapter, I will argue that animals were crucial in medieval mobilities, both material and textual.

### Power of Moving and Feeling: Material Mobility

In the prehistory of interspecies mobility, nonhuman animals made the first moves. Terry O'Connor writes that early in the British postglacial period, perhaps 10,000 years ago, a "mix of temperate large vertebrates" may have established "clearings and 'trails' by grazing and browsing pressure alone. Into this environment, too, came people, drawn by [among other resources]

---

7 *The Etymologies of Isidore of Seville,* trans. Stephen A. Barney et al. (Cambridge: Cambridge University Press, 2006), XII.i.3.

8 John of Trevisa, *On the Properties of Things: John Trevisa's Translation of Bartholomaeus Anglicus De Proprietatibus Rerum, A Critical Text,* gen. ed. Maurice Charles Seymour, 3 vols. (Oxford: Clarendon Press, 1975–1988), XVIII.pro (pp. 1092–93).

9 *Merriam-Webster Dictionary,* s.v. "animal."

the herds of large prey."¹⁰ That is, large animals created paths across a landscape into which they attracted human beings. The new arrivals immediately exerted "predation pressure" on their predecessors, however, and produced new paths and networks.

Human control over the movements of other animals increased and ramified during the British Middle Ages, but the resulting scapes and flows (to use Urry's terminology) were always coproduced. In the following pages, I will sketch three large multispecies movements: importation, management, and collaboration.

*Importation: Trafficked Beasts*

In the first of those movements, animals were objects to be relocated, often for purposes of display. The postglacial landscape into which the "temperate large vertebrates" attracted *Homo sapiens* lacked many species now regarded as endemic.¹¹ Two that now seem particularly British — rabbits and fallow deer — were imported during the Middle Ages for rather surprising reasons. Naomi Sykes and Julie Curl, two British archaeologists, conclude from "the historical, iconographic, zooarchaeological and landscape evidence" that "modern [rabbit] populations descend [...] from individuals brought to Britain" beginning in the twelfth century "as part of a fully-fledged and pan European 'coney culture,'" maintained at great expense by elite households.¹² So too, the motives for transferring fallow deer from the eastern Mediterranean were cultural rather than pragmatic. According to Sykes, "a series of repeated importations" seems to have begun when wealthy Roman colonizers brought small numbers of

---

10 Terry P. O'Connor, "Introduction — The British Fauna in a Changing World," in *Extinctions and Invasions: A Social History of British Fauna*, eds. Terry P. O'Connor and Naomi Jane Sykes, 1–9 (Oxford: Oxbow Books, 2010), 3.

11 "It has long been known," writes Anthony J. Legge, "that South-west Asia is the region of origin for many of our [British] domestic plants and animals" (Anthony J. Legge, "The Aurochs and Domestic Cattle," in O'Connor and Sykes (eds), *Extinctions and Invasions*, 26–35, at 30).

12 Naomi Sykes and Julie Curl, "The Rabbit," in O'Connor and Sykes, eds., *Extinctions and Invasions*, 116–26, at 125.

fallow deer into parks inhabited also by other "exotic" animals, seeking to entertain or impress their guests.[13] Likewise, if Anglo-Saxon rulers imported a few fallow deer, they did so through "peaceful cultural exchange and political negotiation," perhaps "to cement political relationships."[14] Then the Normans did something similar on a larger scale. At the time of the Conquest, deer were still not endemic in Normandy, but they were in Norman Sicily; from there, Norman barons borrowed the "concepts of animal parks," stocking those enclosures with fallow deer and other exotic animals, some of which foreign kings donated to Henry I.[15] Sykes argues that Henry's collection "was a metaphor for the Norman Empire, a statement that the Norman kings had power not only over the wild creatures in their possession but also over the countries from which the animals derived."[16]

*Management: Droves and Enclosures*
As Jennie Friedrich and Sarah Breckenridge Wright point out in essays for this volume, travel can entail both movement and emplacement. That was pre-eminently true for animals trafficked through human cultural and social networks, but a similar binary characterizes their subsequent use. Once imported, many animals were subject to a second kind of control over their mobility: management of independent movement. With rabbits and deer, that management did not mean close restriction.

---

13 Naomi Sykes, "European Fallow Deer," in O'Connor and Sykes, eds., *Extinctions and Invasions,* 51–58, at 52.

14 Ibid., 56.

15 Ibid., 57, citing Willene B. Clark, introd., *A Medieval Book of Beasts* (Woodbridge: Boydell and Brewer, 2006), 18–19. Similarly, Vernon N. Kisling, "Ancient Collections and Menageries," in *Zoo and Aquarium History: Ancient Animal Collections to Zoological Gardens,* ed. Vernon N. Kisling, 1–48 (Boca Raton: CRC Press, 2001), 22.

16 Sykes, "European Fallow Deer," 57. In *Zoo: A History of Zoological Gardens in the West* (London: Reaktion Books, 2002), Eric Baratay and Elisabeth Hardouin-Fugier note that for the pre-modern European aristocracy, as for Roman emperors, wild animals "were considered to be prestigious, luxury items indispensable to the nobility and a symbol of its distinct nature" (17 and 18–19).

On the contrary, such animals were valued for their rapid and agile movement, exercised in warrens and parks. Within those bounds, rabbits and deer were cultivated, while their nonhuman predators were excluded to the extent possible: the aristocratic hunt was a chief objective of non-metaphoric gamekeeping.

The management of other species involved tighter control. Animals that naturally herd together had been managed at least since the late Bronze Age through pastoralism, which provides relatively free but guided movement in search of water and grazing.[17] Indeed, cattle and sheep had long been induced to move substantial distances. Transhumance — seasonal migration between ecological zones — served the welfare of both the animals and their owners; it might be done in stages, with stops for rest and grazing, and it often involved a communal effort.[18]

But two medieval developments changed herd animals' mobility, in opposing ways. The first is evident in a small morphological change: by the late fourteenth century, "drover" joined "driver" as a term for one who "force[s] (living beings) to move on or away."[19] The distinction concerned distance and destination: the "drover" drives herds of cattle "esp. to distant markets."[20] As Hannah Velten writes, large numbers of cattle were brought "along drovers' tracks which criss-crossed [Britain], traveling at about 2 mph for 12 hours a day — the trip from Wales would take 20 to 25 days […]. After such a tremendous journey, the cattle arrived emaciated and were fattened up outside London." Sheep might be driven from as far as Devon (over 200 miles).[21]

---

17 Martyn Allen, "Agriculture and Pastoralism in the Roman West Midlands," Rural Settlement in Britain Project, University of Reading, n.d., https://www.reading.ac.uk/web/FILES/archaeology/West_Midlands_seminar_agriculture_MGA.pdf.

18 See, for instance, M. L. Ryder, "Late Medieval Transhumance in Western Europe," in *Atlas of Medieval Europe*, eds. Angus Mackay and David Ditchburn (London: Routledge, 1997), 219–21.

19 OED s.v. "drive," v. I.iii.a.

20 OED s.v. "drover," n.1.a.; similarly, MED s.vv. "driver(e)" (n.) and "drover(e)" (n.).

21 Hannah Velten, *Beastly London: A History of Animals in the City* (London: Reaktion Books, 2013), 15.

Droves expanded with increasing urbanization; those ending at London's Smithfield Market continued through the nineteenth century, when they were singled out for contributing to the suffering of animals awaiting slaughter.[22] Shirley Toulson suggests that many paths established between Roman times and the eighteenth century were created for and by pack animals and were maintained primarily for drovers;[23] thus constraint in conjunction with movement helped to determine the "scape" of modern Britain.

The mobility of herding animals was controlled also in a second and contrasting way: their grazing ranges were bounded when private and public land-holdings developed. Esther Pascua draws on the "extraordinary sources [that] are available for England for the period 1089–1300" to set forth the changes in animal mobility caused by "the so-called manorial or seigneurial system."[24] Before that period, Pascua explains, domesticated animals in Europe were "roaming property," kept "between the farm and the forest" in forests and natural pastures.[25] By the thirteenth century, however, an "astonishing expansion of arable land" limited the space for animals to roam and graze. Pascua suggests that the resulting "neglect of livestock" may explain why "cows, oxen, pigs, and sheep failed to grow larger during the central centuries of the Middle Ages," otherwise a period of economic growth.[26] The enclosure of fields and the increase in agricultural territory seem to have affected sheep in particular. As Pascua observes, "the manorial shepherd moved his master's fold from place to place within the desmesne" on "the stubble of uncultivated fields after harvest," in order "to fertilize the ex-

---

22  See Diana Donald, "Beastly Sights: The Treatment of Animals as a Moral Theme in Representations of London, c. 1820–1850," *Art History* 22, no. 4 (November 1999): 514–44, at 533 and 539.
23  Shirley Toulson, *The Drovers* (Aylesbury: Shire, 2005), 56.
24  Esther Pascua, "From Forest to Farm and Town: Domestic Animals from ca. 1000 to ca. 1450," in *A Cultural History of Animals: The Medieval Age,* vol. 2, ed. Brigitte Resl, 81–102 (Oxford: Berg, 2007), 89.
25  Ibid., 82, 83, 84.
26  Ibid., 89.

panding fields."²⁷ In a 2009 essay, Lisa J. Kiser reads the fifteenth-century Townley "shepherd plays" in light of these changes.²⁸ Originally tenant farmers with their own sheep, the main characters in those plays have become shepherds who manage their employer's sheep day and night. In the winter, they move the flocks into "the most far-flung corners of the estate" and feed them manually to supplement inadequate grazing.²⁹ Enclosure, a massive but complex determinant of both human and non-human mobility, has visibly transformed the English landscape; one of its components — the management of grazing rights for sheep — is still subject to dispute.³⁰

*Collaboration: Horsepower*

Robin Bendrey points out that animals were involved in land management as both subjects and agents. From early in the first millennium, Bendrey writes, "Horses offered the means of managing territory, cattle and people […], and were therefore the means of controlling wealth and exercising power."³¹

Horses "were present in Early Mesolithic Britain," according to Bendrey, but "became increasingly scarce in the following millennia."³² When humans re-introduced them, probably from the Continent after Britain had been cut off, horses do not seem to have served mostly as sources of food. Their importation was similar in that respect to that of rabbits and deer. In contrast to those creatures, however, horses functioned not as cultural or symbolic goods; rather, they were co-agents in work and war-

---

27 Ibid., 89–90.
28 Lisa J. Kiser, "'Mak's Heirs': Sheep and Humans in the Pastoral Ecology of the Townley First and Second Shepherds' Plays," *JEGP* 108, no. 3 (July 2009): 336–59.
29 Ibid., 349–50.
30 For current discussion of grazing rights in Britain, see for instance the Web site of the Foundation for Common Land (www.foundationforcommonland.org.uk).
31 Robin Bendrey, "The Horse," in O'Connor and Sykes, eds., *Extinctions and Invasions*, 10–16, at 16.
32 Ibid., 10.

fare.³³ In both domains their role has been transformative; they have, in Bendrey's words, "revolutionised transport, warfare, and trade."³⁴ In a major recent study, Pita Kelekna argues that we have underestimated the role of horses in geopolitical and cultural history. "Within anthropology," Kelekna writes,

> cultural advance has traditionally been viewed in the context of the sedentary agricultural state [...]. Analysis of man's symbiosis with the domesticated horse necessarily takes the reader to regions remote from the urban center and pays special attention to mobile elements of nomadic society, too often deemed marginal or transitory [...]. Tribes of [a] vast peripheral area [from Hungary to the borders of China] were notoriously responsible for the depredations and invasions that over millennia threatened the heartlands of civilization to the west, south, and east. [...] [I]t is also true that their far-ranging routes ... afforded rapid transport of distant trade goods, both essential and exotic. With trade went cultural exchange [...].³⁵

Kelekna's research demonstrates that horses have co-produced the most consequential developments in human culture.

In particular ways, horses were crucial in medieval England. As is commonly remarked, etymology renders the so-called Age of Chivalry the "era of the horse"; Middle English *chevalrīe*, meaning interchangeably "host of mounted warriors" and "chivalry" or its "ethical code," descends via Old French from Latin *cabellārius* "horseman."³⁶ In daily life, long-distance transport and communication depended on horses; so, increasingly, did agriculture among peasants as well as the elite.³⁷ Roads and even

---

33 Ibid., 10–13.
34 Ibid., 10.
35 Pita Kelekna, *The Horse in Human History* (Cambridge: Cambridge University Press, 2009), 1.
36 *MED* s.v. "chevalrīe"; *OED* s.vv. "chivalry" (n.) and "cavalry" (n.).
37 John Langdon, "A Quiet Revolution – The Horse in Agriculture, 1100–1500," *History Today* (July 1989): 32–37.

city streets were designed for horse traffic: London's first mayor "decreed that the overhanging projections or jetties on the upper floors of houses had to be at least high enough for a man on horseback to pass under."[38] Chaucer's pilgrims — even the maladept Shipman — take horseback travel for granted. To a large extent, human mobility in the English Middle Ages *was* equine mobility.

Across its medieval functions, what Kelekna aptly calls "man's symbiosis with the domesticated horse" was neither simple nor uniform. Studies by Jeffrey Jerome Cohen and Susan Crane present contrasting models for the aristocratic version of that symbiosis. For Cohen, the relationship between knight and horse in chivalric literature is intimate but dehumanizing: "The horse, its rider, the bridle and saddle and armor together form the Deleuzian circuit or assemblage, a network of meaning that decomposes human bodies and intercuts them with the inanimate, the inhuman."[39] In contrast, Crane emphasizes the representation of horses "as resourceful allies, bold and fearless like their knights."[40] She acknowledges, with Cohen, that the relationship "enmesh[es]" the knight "in a prosthetic assemblage" whose technological aspect "threatens [him] with objectification as just so much equipment," but she insists that it also "carries the knight into a zone of consciousness and an ethical awareness that are not exclusively human."[41] Perhaps both extremes obtained — and not only in aristocratic culture: the plowman and carter, like the knight, probably viewed horses sometimes as transport mechanisms (like themselves) and sometimes as sentient beings (like themselves). Both partners to the "symbiosis" were independent agents powerful enough to exert some control over their mutual mobility.

---

38 Velten, *Beastly London,* 45.
39 Jeffrey Jerome Cohen, *Medieval Identity Machines* (Minneapolis: University of Minnesota Press, 2003), 76.
40 Susan Crane, *Animal Encounters: Contacts and Concepts in Medieval Britain* (Philadelphia: University of Pennsylvania Press, 2013), 143.
41 Ibid., 167.

Admittedly, the balance of control rested more often with the human mover, and the symbiosis lasted only until the human partners found stronger and more biddable forms of "horse power." Medieval rabbits and deer challenged hunters only by human sufferance, and increasing numbers of species were enclosed and managed. Esther Pascua ends her chapter on medieval domestic animals with a summary that applies also to other large mammals. "As the Middle Ages drew to a close," she writes, "working animals were more confined to specific spaces than before, their lives controlled more tightly by human beings. Their fate was determined by the profitability of their activities and products."[42] But at least in medieval England, the *patterns* of human control and movement — in Urry's terminology, the configurations of "complex interlocking networks" and "nodes" along which "people, money, capital, information, ideas and images are seen to 'flow'"[43] — were the work of many species.

*Live Metaphors: Textual Mobility*
Like other new paradigms, John Urry's "mobile sociology" can itself be mobilized in various disciplines. Inspired by Urry's work, Eileen Joy and James L. Smith have proposed that we "consider literary texts themselves [...] as transit systems in which we can glimpse the manifold mobilities of objects, figures, mentalities, tropes and other 'matter' in vibrant intermediate networks."[44] I take that to mean that elements such as metaphors and represented objects exert affective or semiotic force within individual texts and form significant connections beyond those texts. Robert Stanton demonstrates in his essay for this volume that Margery Kempe enacts both kinds of force within and beyond her Book, disrupting expectations for nar-

---

42 Pascua, "From Forest to Farm and Town," 102. Clinton H. Keeling follows the growing list of species in British zoos: "Zoological Gardens of Great Britain" in *Zoo and Aquarium History,* ed. Kisling, 49–74.
43 Urry, *Sociology Beyond Societies,* 12 and 35.
44 Eileen Joy and James L. Smith, "This World Is But a Thurghfare: Transit, Transport, Scapes, and Flows," session proposal, 2014 New Chaucer Society Congress Call for Papers, www.newchaucersociety.org.

rative continuity and genre. In what remains of this chapter, I will argue that nonhuman animals function in a similar way. Indeed, they are particularly "vibrant" objects — and agents — in the "transit systems" of medieval texts.

That proposition might seem untenable, especially because I choose to support it with reference to a genre notorious for representing animals without natural vitality: the medieval beast book, said to be the most widely disseminated form of secular literature from the late classical period through the fifteenth century.[45] Animals are in a sense the co-agents of some modern animal stories — long-haired border collies are among the sources of *Lassie Come-Home* — but medieval animals cannot be regarded as having shaped the bestiary in the same way. Many bestiary creatures are imaginary, for one thing, and some highly improbable behaviors are ascribed to the real ones. Repeated from one bestiary to another, framed by moralizations, the accounts of the animals are more intertextual than zoological. Many commentators argue that bestiary creatures are in fact over-determined, their characteristics dictated contingently by prior texts and ultimately by Christian teleology. Like John Urry when he employs game animals as metaphors, the bestiarists were not really writing about animals, according to this view. Originating from unitary doctrine rather than from observation, confined in a rigid semiotic structure, little changed across innumerable instantiations, the creatures of the texts that we still homogenize as "*the* bestiary" would seem to have brought their literary transit system to a dead halt.

But that is not the impression conveyed by bestiary manuscripts. A great many scribes and artists illustrated their subjects, and their images are anything but static.[46] A frame usually surrounds the creature, just as a verbal moralization might

---

45 Guy R. Mermier, "The Phoenix: Its Nature and Its Place in the Tradition of the Physiologus," in *Beasts and Birds of the Middle Ages: The Bestiary and Its Legacy*, eds. Willene B. Clark and Meradith T. McMunn, 69–87 (Philadelphia: University of Pennsylvania Press, 1989), 70.

46 Florence McCulloch, *Mediaeval Latin and French Bestiaries* (Chapel Hill: University of North Carolina Press, 1960), 70.

enclose a description, but a tail, horn, paw, or beak typically protrudes into or beyond the visual boundary. Sometimes the protrusion substantially invades the text; in British Harley MS 3244 (59r), for instance, the long, slender dragon inside a staggered rectilinear frame stretches from near the top right of the page to the bottom left, interrupting many lines of text.[47] Commenting particularly on the Ashmole bestiary, Debra Hassig describes the effect of this technique: "figures crossing or breaking out of the frame appear more active, as if the frame cannot hold them back." Alternatively, the frame "can encroach upon and effectively hamper the movement of a figure." Hassig sees the latter encroachments as opposing the "breaking out" effect, but in both cases the frame "heighten[s] a sense of movement": escaping or confined, the animal is in motion.[48] Even when not interacting with frames, most bestiary creatures are depicted in motion. "The essential quality of these pictures," observes Beryl Rowland, "is their animation. The animals are presented with such vivacity and vigor that they are oddly compelling, pulsating with life even when grotesque."[49]

Additionally compelling are the creatures' facial expressions. The lion in the Ashmole bestiary looks intent but calm as it consumes a small ape; in another panel, the lion's brows contract as if in anguish as it spares a prostrate man; in a third, it bows to the ground, its mouth half opened, as if in fear of a small cock that wears an improbably haughty expression.[50] Elsewhere, an ape kisses the offspring that she carries before her, her eyes and

---

47 The image is visible in the online Medieval Bestiary, http://bestiary.ca/beasts/beast262.htm.
48 Debra Hassig, "Beauty in the Beasts: A Study of Medieval Aesthetics," RES: Anthropology and Aesthetics 19/20 (1990): 137–61, at 148–49.
49 Beryl Rowland, "The Art of Memory and the Bestiary," in Clark and McMunn (eds), *Beasts and Birds of the Middle Ages,* 12–25, at 17. In that passage, Rowland refers initially to one manuscript (Brussels MS 10066–7) but then generalizes her observation to the sketches that Florence McCulloch made from some two dozen manuscripts (citing McCulloch, *Medieval Latin and French Bestiaries,* 191–212).
50 Facsimile of MS Ashmole 1511 fol. 10r, from http://bodley30.bodley.ox.ac.uk:8180/luna/servlet/s/2saxot.

brow suggesting tenderness. And Christoper De Hamel is right that at least one of the two kids that "[turn] their heads backward to nibble the leaves at the top of a tree" do so "playfully."[51] Perhaps the illustrations' vitality served a mnemonic function, as Rowland maintains, but they strike the viewer first as lively, intentional creatures, not as signposts to particular moralizations.

In that respect, the verbal descriptions match the illustrations: if the creatures described in most beast books are signpoints to moralizations, they are animated, internally motivated ones. Following a scent in the mountains, the lion detects the odor of a hunter, so he covers his tracks with his tail. The *autolops* (antelope? oryx? self-wolf?) is so exceedingly alert that the hunter cannot reach him until he tangles his horns in a spiny shrub. When the *serra* (saw-fish?) sees a sailing ship, he raises his wings in imitation, but he can match the ship's pace for only thirty or forty stadia. Even the igneous rocks are self-moving as well as gendered: they do not ignite unless the male one approaches the female.[52]

Nor do the descriptions themselves stay within a hermeneutic frame. Of the serpent, for instance, we learn that "when he grows old, his eyes become dim and, if he wants to become new again, he abstains and fasts for forty days until his skin becomes loosened from his flesh. And [...] he goes and finds a narrow crack in the rock." The corporeal details in that mini-narrative have no place in the moralization, in which good Christians "throw off for Christ the old man."[53] Moreover, the moral va-

---

51 Christopher De Hamel, ed., *Book of Beasts: A Facsimile of MS Bodley 764* (Oxford: Bodleian Library, 2008), fol. 16v; fol. 36r; p. 29, note to plate 41.
52 *Physiologus Latinus: Éditions Préliminaires*, Versio B, ed. Francis James Carmody (Paris: Librairie E. Droz, 1939), 12–14; my paraphrase is based on Michael J. Curley, trans., *Physiologus* (Chicago: University of Chicago Press, 2009), 1–6. The spelling of "autolops" varies considerably, indicating uncertainty about the creature so designated (McCulloch, *Mediaeval Latin and French Bestiaries*, 85).
53 *Physiologus*, trans. Curley, 16. Curley's base text is a manuscript from the stemma known as Versio y (see Curley, xxxiii). My summaries here include his interpolations from the elaborations in Versio b, which is said to be

lences of some figurations are surprising: we expect poisonous serpents to represent something evil, for instance, not the good Christian. Often a creature's moral valence shifts polarity, as the author acknowledges after declaring that the caladrius "stands for the person of our Savior." "Perhaps you say that the caladrius is unclean according to the law," he writes, but so too the unclean serpent was exalted by Moses just as "the son of man should be exalted" (alluding to John 3:14); indeed, "there are many other things in creatures that have two meanings; some are indeed to be praised, others to be blamed."[54]

Thus both parts of the description/signification pair are internally complex. Indeed, the two-fold semiotic structure is less a general rule than a ground for variation. In some beast books, many chapters have no moralization at all.[55] More commonly, significations abound, intertwining with the descriptions that generate them. An extreme instance of such chaining is the self-similar explication of the oyster and pearl that comes midway through Versio y of the *Physiologus* as translated by Michael J. Curley. We learn first of the agate-stone that divers use to find pearls. Without pausing for moralization, the author moves to the pearl itself, born when the "stone in the sea called oyster" (*sostoros*) swallows the light and dew of celestial bodies. The agate, we are told, corresponds to St. John, who showed "that the intelligible pearl is Jesus Christ our Lord," who is brought up from the sea of the world by "holy doctors." And although sinners/divers carry the pearl back down, the Savior is "found intelligibly receiving food […] in the middle of the shell" — that is, between the Old and New Testaments.[56] The "stone which is

"particularly well represented by English MSS of the thirteenth century" (Eden, ed. and trans., *Theobaldi "Physiologus,"* 3). The serpent is not in Versio b but appears in Versio y and in the early, versified "Physiologus" attributed to one Theobaldus and believed to have been used as a school text; see *Physiologus,* trans. Curley, 103.

54 *Physiologus Latinus,* ed. Carmody, 15–16 (my translation).
55 Clark, Introduction to *Medieval Book of Beasts,* 115; McCulloch, *Mediaeval Latin and French Bestiaries,* 35.
56 The segment of the oyster/pearl passage summarized after this point is absent from Versio y and from Carmody's edition of Versio b; Curley trans-

called the conch" is (also?) a figure for Holy Mary, who rose, like the stone from the sea, out of her father's house to receive the dew of Gabriel's annunciation, foreshadowed in Genesis 27:28 — "May God give you of the dew of heaven"; the "opening of the mouth of the conch" indicates Mary's receptive reply to the Angel, in Luke 1:38. Two scriptural elaborations of the Incarnation follow before we move to the "pearl of great price" (Matthew 13:46), itself explicated through ten additional Bible passages that confirm the value of the figurative pearl. At this point, after four full pages (in the translated version), the writer would seem to have lost sight of his first metaphoric vehicle. But he brings us back to the adamant-stone with a short chapter on its other "nature," the imperviousness that confers power on its owners. And this time, the *significatio* is brief and direct, closing the circumlocution: "My Lord is adamant-rock. If you possess him, no evil will befall you."[57]

If the animals in such texts are fundamentally "vehicle[s] for understanding religious truth," as Joyce Salisbury claims,[58] the oyster and pearl are rather inefficient ones, linked as they are to multiple biblical passages whose meanings are already explicit. It makes better sense to see them as semiotic engines. The scriptural and didactic significations that they generate outweigh them in authority, but rhetorical agency belongs to the creatures that call them forth. The relationship is beautifully figured in two illustrations that Hugh of Fouilloy designed for his *De avibus*.[59] In one, a dove is encircled by a segmented ring and a rectangle containing small circles. Those circles, the segments, and

---

lates it from a fragment designated as B1, published in an 1888 article by Max Friedrich Mann, "Der Bestiaire Divin des Guillaume le Clerc" (available through Google at https://ia802503.us.archive.org/33/items/DerBestiaireDivinMann/Der_Bestiaire_Divin_Mann.pdf). My information about the pearl, agate-stone, and oyster in Versio y is from McCulloch, *Mediaeval Latin and French Bestiaries*, 154–55.

57 *Physiologus*, trans. Curley, 34–38.
58 Joyce E. Salisbury, *The Beast Within: Animals in the Middle Ages* (New York: Routledge, 1994), 110.
59 Willene B. Clark, "The Illustrated Medieval Aviary and the Lay-Brotherhood," *Gesta* 21, no. 1 (1982): 63–74, at 64. Clark argues that Hugh designed

a space between two borders all contain phrases from Hugh's scriptural and homiletic explication of the dove. A falcon occupies the center of the other illustration, enclosed by a double-lined rectangle with double-lined arms that quadrisect the outer area; the inner spaces and outer segments contain text with "a few essential ideas" concerning the falcon.[60] The diagrams reverse the usual relationship between central text and marginal image in medieval manuscripts: here, discourse emanates in various directions from the animal at its center.

The dove recurs in many beast books, seldom generating exactly the same significations. The authors draw on a large stock of features and behaviors, some with Biblical warrant, some derived from Isidore of Seville's *Etymologies* or Alexander Neckam's *De naturis rerum,* and a few attested by observation: "I have found no written reference to the colour of the dove's wings, but it can be attributed by analogy with the material dove (*ex similitudine materialis columbe*)."[61] Through many variations, including its material form, the creature being described remains the same — the dove, subject to interpretation but not completely knowable.

The generative power of bestiary creatures extends beyond the bestiaries. Predictably, bestiary descriptions and significations appear in sermons, but they also migrate to beast epics, fables, debate poems, travel narratives, and even romances.[62]

---

the diagrams himself. She reproduces them, from BN MS lat. 2495 and Douai, Bibl. Mun. MS 370, on p. 65.

60 Clark, "Illustrated Medieval Aviary," 69.
61 "Transcription and Translation," *Aberdeen Bestiary,* 28v; similarly, Hugh of Fouilloy in Clark, "Illustrated Medieval Aviary," ch. 7 (131).
62 For overlap between the bestiary and the beast epic, see Elaine C. Block and Kenneth Varty, "Choir-Stall Carvings of Reynard and Other Foxes," in *Reynard the Fox: Social Engagement and Cultural Metamorphoses in the Beast Epic from the Middle Ages to the Present,* ed. Varty, 125–62 (New York: Berghahn Books, 2000), 150–51. Thomas Honegger connects the fables of Robert Henryson and (briefly) John Lydgate with bestiaries in "Legacy of the Bestiaries," 53–65. Several commentators see bestiary echoes in The Owl and the Nightingale — for instance, Jill Mann, *From Aesop to Reynard: Beast Literature in Medieval Britain* (Oxford: Oxford University Press, 2009), 156–60. Anthony Paul Bale points out many bestiary parallels in the intro-

Those reappearances demonstrate the influence of the bestiary, but I would argue that they also exemplify the mobility of the creatures themselves. For literary animals do not merely migrate across genre barriers; they trample them. At least three scholars observe that readers often ignore or misidentify the genres of texts that center on animals. Clark writes that modern commentators exaggerate the popularity of bestiaries because they use the term 'bestiary' "for any animal lore in text or art."[63] Jill Mann makes a similar observation, though for her the overused term isn't "bestiary" but "fable"; thus Mann opens her masterful book on beast literature in medieval Britain with a remedial lesson on genre distinctions.[64] And the tendencies deplored by Clark and Mann are generalized in a trenchant observation at the beginning of Jan Ziolkowski's study of medieval Latin beast poetry. "When authors or readers are confronted with an animal protagonist," writes Ziolkowski, "they are inclined automatically to think of other types of literature about animals, regardless of whether those other types are in the same genre. The moral of the story is that beasts override genre."[65]

If they can do that, literary animals share a power possessed by entities at the opposite end of the ontological scale — that is, by sin, virtue, the trinity, and other elements of Christian doctrine. For many readers, allusions to those theological realities dominate any lyric, epic, fable, or narrative in which they emerge, pulling the text into a supercategory that some call "allegory." Like allegory, the supergenre that we might call "beast literature" is established not simply by a shared theme or subject-matter but by a particular rhetorical stance toward its

---

duction and notes to his edition and translation of "Mandeville's travels": *The Book of Marvels and Travel* (Oxford: Oxford University Press, 2012). For connections with romances, see Meradith T. McMunn, "Bestiary Influences in Two Thirteenth-Century Romances," in *Beasts and Birds of the Middle Ages*, 134–50.

63 Clark, Introduction to *Medieval Book of Beasts*, 13.
64 Mann, *From Aesop to Reynard*, 1.
65 Jan M. Ziolkowski, *Talking Animals: Medieval Latin Beast Poetry, 750–1150*, (Philadelphia: University of Pennsylvania Press, 1993), 1.

shared subject-matter. Fables, bestiary entries, beast epics, avian debate poems, and modern animal fiction all present their animal agents as members of real species — a rooster, the serpent, the dove, my dog. As signifieds, both beasts and the sacred are existentially real but beyond full human comprehension. Thus they act as semiotic magnets. They produce what Urry might call "flows," attracting and resignifying figures and themes within individual texts and among texts that are otherwise diverse. Inevitably, of course, readers recognize that the representation of a species in a particular text falls short of mimesis, producing what might be called animal nominalism. Genres differ in their characteristic strategies for subverting and acknowledging that shortfall; texts (and readings of texts) differ in their fluctuating distances from the animal real. But if we ignore that movement — by, for instance, defining the action in fables and the descriptions in bestiaries as expendable fabrication — we de-animate the texts.

## Conclusion: Our Move

As I read about "mobile sociology," I thought of Stephen Glosecki's essay on early Germanic animal imagery. "Striking creatures stare across the centuries at us," writes Glosecki, "blankly indifferent to our urge to understand [...]. Literally, many were movable goods back then; figuratively, they cross historical boundaries, too, with whispers of ways forgotten."[66] Indeed, medieval animals were literally — that is, materially — movable objects, but as Glosecki's rhetoric implies, they were also moved and moving agents. The "ways" that they both followed and produced have left traces on the British landscape, from half-vanished drovers' roads to the invisible plot lines of medieval deer parks within which wild fallow deer still live.[67]

---

66 Stephen O. Glosecki, "Movable Beasts: The Manifold Implications of Early Germanic Animal Imagery," in *Animals in the Middle Ages: A Book of Essays,* ed. Nona C. Flores, 3–23 (New York: Garland, 1996), 15 and 17.

67 Naomi Sykes writes that although deer parks "fell into disrepair" early in the twentieth century, the "current distribution" of fallow deer "is remarkably

And co-mobility itself is by no means an historical artifact. Human mobility today relocates far more living things than the exotic mammals trafficked by our distant ancestors. Elizabeth Kolbert reports that some "ten thousand different species are being moved around the world just in ballast water" during any twenty-four-hour period, for instance, and that in one summer, tourists and researchers to Antarctica "brought with them more than seventy thousand seeds from other continents."[68] Organisms of all kinds have invaded territories where they were not previously known, often producing competition, genetic change, and occasional extinction. "We are," writes Kolbert, "in effect, reassembling the world into one enormous supercontinent — what biologists sometimes refer to as the New Pangaea."[69] The effects on particular species are under widespread investigation, but "biotic homogenization" inevitably involves all creatures, including homo sapiens, in a network of change.[70]

If a parallel "cultural homogenization" is taking place, as some maintain, the figurative beasts of the Middle Ages may be among the most successful invading species.[71] Modern bestiaries abound: as of March, 2015, Barnes & Noble offers 379 products titled "bestiary," including collections of modern and contemporary poems (by Guillaume Apollinaire, Ted Hughes, Elise Paschen, and many others), music albums (a dozen of them, the most recent from the "left-field hip-hop supergroup 'Hail Mary

---

similar to Rackham's [...] plot of medieval parks" (Sykes, "European Fallow Deer," 52, citing O. Rackham, *The History of the Countryside* [London: Phoenix, 1997], 124).

68 Elizabeth Kolbert, *The Sixth Extinction: An Unnatural History* (New York: Henry Holt, 2014), 198 and 207.

69 Ibid., 208.

70 "The anthropogenic reshuffling of the earth's biota has resulted in taxonomic homogenization, irrespective of taxonomic group and spatial scale" (B. Baiser et al., "Pattern and Process of Biotic Homogenization in the New Pangaea," *Proceedings of the Royal Society B: Biological Sciences* 279, no. 1748 [December 7, 2012]: 4772–77).

71 "Cultural homogenization" seems to be used freely without attribution, but scholars associate the phrase and concept with the work of Ernest Gellner, Jürgen Habermas, and Wolfgang Welsch.

Mallon'"), an "artist's guide to creating mythical creatures" (William O'Connor's *Dracopedia: The Bestiary*), a self-published cultural commentary (Rori O'Keeffe's *My Little Blue Bestiary,* with chapters on "The Fire-Breathing Lesbian" and "The Long-Nosed Neighbor"), and serious studies of animals in a particular culture (Thailand, Siam, or J. R. R. Tolkien's Middle-earth). There is even a charming *Punctuation Bestiary* (by Kiran Spees) featuring the Exclamatore and the Punctuation Rabbits. Few of those products appear to be about animals; if they allude to medieval bestiaries at all, they do so under the assumption that those too had little to do with actual beasts. Of course, that assumption is shared by scholars who argue that the existential reality of bestiary animals did not matter: the animals' role "was to provide metaphors or symbols for a variety of Christian mandates and beliefs."[72] If that were true, bestiary animals would always have been homogenized by the cultural systems that they invade, perhaps so thoroughly that they would bear little resemblance to biological conspecifics.

I do not know how true that is of the denizens of modern bestiaries. But I can attest that their medieval precursors derive one crucial feature from what can be called the Animal Real: locomotion. Illustrated in action, gesturing through painted borders, bestiary creatures carry diverse significations into multiple texts without regard to genre. As centers of metaphoric interpretation, they precede metaphor and remain demonstrably apart from it. As Lesley Kordecki points out, variant figurae produce "indeterminacy [...] that arises out of the knowledge of the verbal game afoot at the very core of the bestiary."[73] Like

---

72 Pamela Gravestock, "Did Imaginary Animals Exist?," in *The Mark of the Beast: The Medieval Bestiary in Art, Life, and Literature,* ed. Debra Hassig, 119–39 (New York: Garland, 1999), 130. Similarly, Ron Baxter, *Bestiaries and Their Users in the Middle Ages* (Stroud: Sutton, 1998), 72, and Mann, *From Aesop to Reynard*, 161. Gravestock goes on to qualify the statement that I quote above, writing that some of the imaginary creatures are not moralized (130–31).

73 Lesley Kordecki, "Making Animals Mean: Speciest Hermeneutics in the Physiologus of Theobaldus," in *Animals in the Middle Ages,* 85–101, at 94.

Glosecki's intersubjective zoomorphs, literary beasts participate in semiotic networks, but they also pull us out of interpretation altogether, onto the presymbolic terrain that we share with other living creatures.

5

# Building Bridges to Canterbury

*Sarah Breckenridge Wright*

In 2015, the word *listicle* was added to OxfordDictionaries.com, defined as "an article on the Internet presented in the form of a numbered or bullet-pointed list."[1] By consulting a listicle, one can learn "16 Snapchats Only Hipsters Would Send" (all deeply ironic) and "25 Things You Should Learn To Do Before Turning 25" (including "say no sometimes" and "invert the color on your phone for reading at night").[2] While the listicle is a relatively new phenomenon, it belies humankind's longstanding desire to classify and categorize the world around it. The hipsters, steampunks, and rockabillies of the twenty-first century were born of the same categorizing impulse that generated the beasts, birds, and serpents of the medieval bestiary. While this impulse ostensibly helps us understand the world, it too often leads to dichotomies that fail to capture the dynamism of humankind and the world we inhabit.[3]

---

1 *Oxford Dictionaries Online*, s.v. "listicle, n.," http://www.oxforddictionaries.com.
2 This medievalist, enamored by the materiality of books, takes issue with the latter.
3 One might recall the categorizing impulse that leads John Urry to render animals metaphoric vehicles rather than social agents in *Sociology beyond Societies,* discussed in Carolynn Van Dyke's "Animal Vehicles: Mobility beyond Metaphor" in the present collection.

The current essay seeks to explore two dichotomies inimical to the fields of cultural geography and ecocriticism: nature vs. culture, and mobility vs. stasis. Specifically, I will present the medieval bridge as an icon of hybridity: a cultural artifact that commingles human/animal movement, architectural stasis, and the natural world (blood, stone, and water), and in so doing bears witness to the profound hybridity of the Middle Ages. I will then briefly explore how the underlying presence of medieval bridges in the frame narrative of Chaucer's *Canterbury Tales* suggests an emerging category of geographically-determined identity in the fourteenth century, one that lies somewhere between the early medieval dependence on the physical landscape and early modernity.[4] These explorations will, I hope, serve as models for identifying hybrid spaces and identities — at once human and nonhuman, mobile and static — in literatures and landscapes in and beyond the medieval.

The first of the two dichotomies this essay explores — nature vs. culture — has long been the subject of ecocritical conversations. In its inception, ecocriticism sought to reclaim nature as something more than the backdrop for human action. Once reserved for texts explicitly about the nonhuman (e.g. nature writing), the field has begun to consider literature that is not consciously about nature, combining principles of literary theory and ecology to critique anthropocentric narratives. Michael McDowell observes that Bakhtinian dialogics, for example, "[help] first by placing an emphasis on contradictory voices, rather than focusing mainly upon the authoritative monologic voice of the narrator. We begin to hear characters and elements of the land-

---

4 See Clare A. Lees and Gillian R. Overing, eds., *A Place to Believe in: Locating Medieval Landscapes* (University Park: Pennsylvania State University Press, 2006); Scott Smith, *Land and Book: Literature and Land Tenure in Anglo-Saxon England* (Toronto: University of Toronto Press, 2012). I also explore this phenomenon in "The Soil's Holy Bodies: The Art of Chorography in William of Malmesbury's Gesta Pontificum Anglorum," *Studies in Philology* 111, no. 4 (2014): 652–79.

scape that have been marginalized."[5] Though McDowell speaks in large part of nature writing, Rebecca M. Douglass notes that his observations help us "imagine a dialogics that might recover the still more silent voice of the land in *other* texts as well."[6] Such imaginings have produced a plethora of helpful questions we can ask of the "other," moving ecocriticism from the purview of Barbara Kingsolver to Henry James, modern to medieval.[7]

Scholars of the Middle Ages in particular have made great strides in asking and answering such questions, moving ecocriticism beyond contemporary nature writing by considering how the field offers a new lens on medieval literature and culture.[8] In his foundational essay "The Historical Roots of Our Ecological Crisis," Lynn White Jr. suggests that the seventh-century scratch plow fundamentally changed humankind's relationship to the earth, observing that "the distribution of land was based no longer on the needs of a family but, rather, on the capacity of

---

5 Michael McDowell, "The Bakhtinian Road to Ecological Insight," in *The Ecocriticism Reader: Landmarks in Literary Ecology,* eds. Cheryll Glotfelty and Harold Fromm (Athens: University of Georgia Press, 1996), 373.
6 Rebecca M. Douglass, "Ecocriticism and Middle English Literature," *Studies in Medievalism* 10 (1998): 136–63, at 141. Emphasis mine.
7 On ecocriticism and Henry James, see Kathleen R. Wallace and Karla Armbruster's introduction to *Beyond Nature Writing: Expanding the Boundaries of Ecocriticism* (Charlottesville: University Press of Virginia, 2001).
8 See, for example: Lynn White Jr., "The Historical Roots of Our Ecological Crisis" in *The Ecocriticism Reader,* 3–14; Lisa J. Kiser, "Chaucer and the Politics of Nature," in *Beyond Nature Writing,* 41–56 (Charlottesville: University Press of Virginia, 2001); Sarah Stanbury, "Ecochaucer: Green Ethics and Medieval Nature," *The Chaucer Review* 39, no. 1 (2004): 1–16; Gillian Rudd, *Greenery: Ecocritical Readings of Late Medieval English Literature* (Manchester: Manchester University Press, 2010); Alfred K. Siewers, *Strange Beauty: Ecocritical Approaches to Early Medieval Landscape* (New York: Palgrave Macmillan, 2009); Karl Steel, *How To Make a Human: Animals and Violence in the Middle Ages* (Columbus: Ohio State University Press, 2011); Jeffrey Jerome Cohen, *Stone: An Ecology of the Inhuman* (Minneapolis: University of Minnesota Press, 2015). See also Jeffrey Jerome Cohen's edited collections: *Animal, Mineral, Vegetable: Ethics and Objects* (Brooklyn: punctum books, 2012), *Prismatic Ecology: Ecotheory beyond Green* (Mineapolis: University of Minnesota Press, 2013), and Lowell Duckert, "Ecomaterialisms," special issue of *postmedieval: a journal of medieval cultural studies* 4, no. 1 (2013).

a power machine to till the earth [...]. Formerly man had been part of nature; now he was the exploiter of nature."⁹ This observation justified and made necessary medieval ecocritique, locating the origin story of our ecological crisis in the Middle Ages, and tacitly encouraging literary critics to look for evidence of this crisis in the period's literature. Douglass responded by providing a veritable "medieval ecocritic's tool belt," rethinking ecocritical terminology in the Middle Ages ("nature," for example), and listing questions one might ask of a medieval text, while Lisa J. Kiser and Sarah Stanbury pose such questions of Chaucer, whose *Canterbury Tales* serves as the literary model of hybridity in the present essay. Each examination in its own way suggests that ecocriticism no longer belongs exclusively to the Muirs and Whitmans of our world.¹⁰

In all cases, medieval and modern, the challenge is to not ignore culture in the same way that ecocritics suggest extant criticism ignores nature; in other words, to not perpetuate the nature-culture dichotomy. This danger is acknowledged by Kathleen R. Wallace and Karla Ambruster in their collection *Beyond Nature Writing,* where they write, "we believe that a continued focus on nature and wilderness writing within ecocriticism might reinforce this same nature-culture dualism while, this time, privileging nature over culture."¹¹ Sven Birkirts echoes this sentiment, writing, "Nature and its preservation is what occupies most of the ecocritics. And this imposes a kind of programmatic simplicity upon the whole movement [...] . How much more interesting and controversial would be an ecocriticism pledging itself to the more inclusive idea of 'environment.'"¹² So, reading anthropocentric narrative through an ecocritical lens is certainly a step in the right direction, but we might also rethink

---

9   White, "The Historical Roots of Our Ecological Crisis," 3.
10  This is said, of course, with nothing but love for Muir and Whitman.
11  Wallace and Armbruster, "Introduction: Why Go Beyond Nature Writing and Where To?" 4.
12  Sven Birkert, "Only God Can Make a Tree: The Joys and Sorrows of Ecocriticism," *Boston Book Review* 3, no. 1 (1996), n.p., http://www.asle.org/wp-content/uploads/ASLE_Primer_Birkerts.pdf.

the terminology and theory that drives ecocriticism, adopting more holistic vocabulary and exploring systems/networks that more accurately represent our hybrid world. Even when reclaiming the nonhuman landscape's marginalized voice in monologic narrative, the ecocritic must be careful not to disallow the presence and impact of human culture. As William Howarth writes, "although we cast nature and culture as opposites, in fact they constantly mingle, like water and soil in a flowing stream."[13]

The current essay seeks to demonstrate the aptness of Howarth's stream simile by turning to the structures that traverse and are embedded in streams: the inclusive 'environments' of medieval bridges. And while all bridges warrant ecocritique, I turn to those of the Middle Ages because the period's hybridity reinforces the need to escape binaristic thought. In the late fourteenth century, conflicts of church and state, and demographic and economic flux destabilized national and regional identities defined by geographical fixity.[14] The period is remarkable instead for its mobility. Faith, disease, and bourgeoning commercial exploits propelled bodies across the world, and literature recorded this movement, with Chaucer's *Canterbury Tales* serving as an exemplary model of how medieval texts contended with hybrid understandings of space and identity. Like John and Aleyn in the *Reeve's Tale*, who pass "a brook, and over that a brigge" in search of fruitful economic (and sexual) exchange (1.3922), real and imagined medieval bodies yielded to the ebbs and flows of

---

13  William Howarth, "Some Principles of Ecocriticism," in *The Ecocriticism Reader,* 69–91, at 69. As Vin Narduzzi notes in his review essay on medieval ecocriticism, Karl Steel advocates for this escape from binarism in his epilogue, wherein he suggests humans must "abandon themselves to relationships unavailable to mere animals or, for that matter, to mere humans, whether medieval or modern" (Steel, quoted in Vin Narduzzi, "Medieval ecocriticism," *postmedieval* 4, no. 1 [2013]: 112–23, at 120).

14  One may recall that the fourteenth century saw the Hundred Years' War, political strife that led to the War of the Roses, the Papal Schism, *and* the Black Death. As Paul Strohm notes in *Chaucer's Tale: 1386 and the Road to Canterbury* (New York: Viking, 2014), Chaucer's refrain — "to maken virtue of necessitee" — was very likely a reaction to blows of fate that rendered his life/times a series of "crises."

an increasingly mobile world, encountering bridges en route that were shaped in and from the natural world that they, in turn, transformed.[15]

## Bridging Liquid Landscapes

Bridges themselves, before we consider the more inclusive environment of which they are a part, are emblematic of hybridity, representing both site and transition. As such, they deconstruct the familiar geographical dichotomy that sets mobility against stasis, the second of two dichotomies that this essay explores. Since the introduction of the "new mobilities paradigm," geographers have discussed mobility in opposition to sedentarism. Mimi Sheller and John Urry observe, "The emergent mobilities paradigm [...] undermines sedentarist theories present in many studies in geography, anthropology, and sociology. Sedentarism treats as normal stability, meaning, and place, and treats as abnormal distance, change, and placelessness."[16] Movement is set against stasis, place against placelessness, and, in some criticism, illusion against reality (where "the stationary state is only fiction").[17] Book-length considerations of mobility focus largely on transport or the socio-political implications of and impact on moving bodies/things, and the built environment (like "nature" in the nature-culture dichotomy) is rendered "backdrop."[18] Ulf

---

15  All quotations taken from *The Riverside Chaucer,* ed. Larry D. Benson, 3rd ed. (Cambridge: Harvard University Press, 1987). Quotations will be cited by fragment and line number.

16  See Mimi Sheller and John Urry, "The New Mobilities Paradigm," *Environment and Planning* 38 (2006): 207–26 at 208.

17  Walter Christaller, *Central Places in Southern Germany* (London: Prentice-Hall, 1966), 84. On the reality/fiction of movement/stasis, see also Henri Bergson, *Matter and Memory* (New York: Macmillan, 1950).

18  Some of the best studies on the subject include: Tim Cresswell, *On the Move: Mobility in the Modern Western World* (New York: Routledge, 2006); *Mobilities, Networks, Geographies,* eds. Jonas Larsen, John Urry, and Kay Axhausen (Aldershot: Ashgate, 2006); Peter Adey, *Mobility* (New York: Routledge, 2010); Margaret Grieco and John Urry, eds., *Mobilities: New Perspectives on Transport and Society* (Aldershot: Ashgate, 2011); and Tim Cresswell and Peter Merriman, eds., *Geographies of Mobilities: Practices,*

Strohmayer observes of existing mobility studies, "architecture forms at best an assumed and largely stable set of geographical nodes into which [...] mobilities are thrust" (119).[19] The problem that emerges is a consequent association of architecture with determination and mobility with personal agency, which renders the former adverse to a society that celebrates free will, and unattractive to scholars more excited by the enigmatic.

Yet there may be room for a geographical reality that is *both* stable *and* changing, especially in a period when geographically constructed identities were only just evolving from place-based understandings (i.e. the Middle Ages). Peter Adey allows for this possibility in his discussion of airport vectors. Rather than accepting airports as fixed entities or nodes through which bodies/things move, he argues that airports are *made from* lines of mobility.[20] He writes, "Passenger mobilities are treated indivisibly. They are imagined as flows and rivers and, thus, modeled as vectors that eventually become real in the 'real' material environment of the terminal. Lines and flows materialise into the tube like structures of gates, tunnels, and corridors — the materialisation of what [Gilles] Deleuze and [Félix] Guattari would know as hydraulic science."[21] In this way, vectors are materialized, allowing for the physical manifestation of mobility in the

---

*Spaces, Subjects* (Aldershot: Ashgate, 2013). Though I present a call for hybrid understanding here, I in no way mean to denigrate the very important work of these scholars.

19 Ulf Strohmayer, "Bridges: Different Conditions of Mobile Possibilities," in *Geographies of Mobilities: Practices, Spaces, Subjects,* eds. Tim Cresswell and Peter Merriman, 119–35 (Aldershot: Ashgate, 2013), 119. Strohmayer follows this observation with a list of scholars who are taking steps toward theoretical and empirical appraisals of the built environment, including Peter Kraftl and Loretta Lees.

20 On airports as fixed and/or nodes, see Peter Adey, "Airports and Air-Mindedness: Spacing, Timing, and Using Liverpool Airport 1929–39," *Social and Cultural Geography* 7 (2006): 343–63; M. Crang, "Between Places: Producing Hubs, Flows, and Networks," *Environment and Planning A* 34 (2002): 569–74.

21 Peter Adey, "Airports: Terminal/Vector," in *Geographies of Mobilities,* eds. Cresswell and Merriman, 140. (This is one of many essays in which Adey discusses the results of his research at Liverpool Airport.)

"real" landscape. Architecture becomes capricious, bending to the networks that move through and across it.

Because the construction of bridges is both literally and figuratively a consequence of hydraulics, we might think of bridges as vectors, "inseparable from flows [...] and heterogen[eous], as opposed to the stable, the eternal, the identical, the constant."[22] They are the architectural manifestation of movement, engendering and engendered by mobile practice. Indeed, bridges are more likely to fall into disrepair and collapse when bodies cease to move across them, and the temporary absence of a bridge that makes movement possible can be a remarkably disruptive event in the urban history of a city.[23]

The hybridity of the structure itself, at once static and mobile, is echoed by the bodies that occupy it. When standing on a bridge, one is "there" (i.e., emplaced) primarily because one is between places. This dynamism becomes particularly acute when we consider the living bridges of the Middle Ages. A body can *loiter* on a road, but it can *live* on a medieval bridge.[24] In 1281 a royal writ concerning London Bridge mentions "almost innumerable people dwelling thereon," and a rental survey of Bridge House properties in 1358 shows that there were 62 shops on the east side of the roadway and 69 on the west side.[25] The bridge was therefore far more than a determining structure, facilitating or impeding river crossings; it was a place of residence and economic exchange, a microcosm of the city suspended over the

---

22 Gilles Deleuze and Felix Guattari, *A Thousand Plateaus: Capitalism and Schizophrenia*, trans. Brian Massumi (London: Athlone Press, 1987), 361.
23 As a resident of Pittsburgh — the "City of Bridges" — the latter strikes especially close to home.
24 On medieval roads (which provide a productive comparison to medieval bridges), see Valerie Allen, "Roads," *postmedieval* 4, no. 1 (2013): 18–29.
25 *Calendar of Patent Rolls* preserved in the Public Record Office, 65 vols. (London: 1291–1509, 1547–63, 1893–1948); C. Welch, *History of Tower Bridge* (London: 1894), 258–59. Quoted in Bruce Watson, Trevor Brigham, and Tony Dyson, *London Bridge: 2000 Years of a River Crossing* (London: Museum of London Archeology Service, 2001), 97–98.

Thames.[26] Beyond the momentous historical events played out thereupon (the Peasants' Revolt, for example), daily life would have consisted of innumerable micro and macro movements: blood flowing in veins and in streets as fish were butchered, money being exchanged for goods, estranged hearts being exchanged to signify shifting allegiances,[27] and bodies flocking toward the chapel of St Thomas the Martyr or a *tableau vivant* at the Southwark Bridge foot. In sum, the medieval bridge is a picture of post-modern consumption, a vector of mobility-supporting networks, producing and presupposing extensive new mobilities.[28] Both the built structure and the bodies occupying it are therefore fundamentally hybrid: mobile and stable, emplaced and between places.

The way medieval bridges were built compounds their failure to preserve binary opposition. Extant records suggest that as early as the Anglo-Saxon period, bridge construction and maintenance was a common burden.[29] This burden — originally one of Alfred's *trinoda necessitas* — improved defense and communication, making bridges central to enabling (and disabling, in the case of invasion) the movement of bodies and ideas, the latter including a burgeoning sense of nationalism that came from early defensive efforts against the Vikings. In this way, the act of bridge construction united people across space and estate in a shared architectural project that enabled collective routines including trade, pilgrimage, and the performance of civic duties. In so doing, bridges produced and came to represent new itinerant identities, uprooting "Englishness" from the soil and locating it instead in mobile categories.

---

26 London Bridge as both connection and barrier (the latter as a consequence of the gates thereon: the Stonegate and the Drawbridge Gate), reveals yet another sense in which medieval bridges can be read as hybrid.

27 See Jennie Friedrich's "*Concordia Discors*: The Traveling Heart as Foreign Object in Chaucer's *Troilus and Criseyde*" in the present collection.

28 On bridges as spaces of post-modern consumption, see David Harrison, *The Bridges of Medieval England: Transport and Society 400–1800* (Oxford: Clarendon Press, 2004); Alan Cooper, *Bridges, Law, and Power in Medieval England, 700–1400* (Woodbridge: Boydell, 2006).

29 See Cooper, *Bridges, Law, and Power in Medieval England*, ch. 2.

The Rochester Bridge was one of the most important bridge projects in all of England, carrying Watling Street over the Medway, and thereby linking London to both Canterbury and the Continent. After the original medieval bridge (constructed ca. 960 CE) succumbed to the force of ice melts in 1381, Sir Robert Knolles, Sir John Cobham, and architect Henry Yevele spearheaded the construction of a second bridge.[30] The importance of this bridge to Rochester, and Southeast England, cannot be overstated. From its beginning, Rochester was defined by its proximity to and contention with the Medway, its Roman name being *Durobrivis*: a compound of two Celtic words meaning "walled town by the bridge." The construction of the 560-foot 1391 bridge reinforced this link, serving as the most frequently used Medway crossing for nearly 500 years.[31] Upon its completion, it was called "sumptuoissimus" (most magnificent) by Thomas of Walsingham, and as late as the eighteenth century, it was praised by Daniel Defoe as "the largest, highest, and the strongest built of all bridges in England, except London Bridge."[32] Throughout its literary record, the bridge's place in southeast England was secured by superlatives.

Nonetheless, the Rochester Bridge, more than most pieces of architecture, was *itself* a body in motion. This essay has already explored the theoretical hybridity of bridges as vectors, and the extension of this hybridity to the bodies that occupy them, but a material turn reveals that bridges are anything but static architectural structures. This is in large part due to the rivers in which

---

30 The author of the *Westminister Chronicle* writes, "About the feast of the Purification of the Blessed Virgin this year a great part of Rochester Bridge was destroyed. Ice had formed in vast quantities, and when it broke up, with the onset of milder weather, the massive pressure of the flores [sic] which had composed it wrecked the bridge" (*The Westminister Chronicle, 1381–1394*, eds. L.C. Hector and B.F. Harvey [Oxford: Oxford Medieval Texts, 1982], 2–3).

31 It was replaced in 1856 with a bridge that better accommodated modern river traffic.

32 Thomas Walsingham, *Historia Anglicana,* ed. H.T. Riley, Rolls ser., vol. 2 (London: 1863–4), 277; Daniel Defoe, *Tour Thro' the Whole Island of Great Britain* (London: 1724), 20.

they are embedded and the raw materials with which they are made: a reminder that an understanding of bridges is incomplete without an analysis of the natural world, bringing Birkirt's notion of inclusive environments to the fore and colliding the mobility-stasis and nature-culture dichotomies. In the case of Rochester Bridge, nature was commingled with culture from the bridge's inception. Keeping the original medieval bridge's collapse in mind, planners chose to locate the 1391 bridge one hundred feet further upriver, "both for the fastnes of the soile and for the breaking of the swiftness of the streame."[33] Already soil and water were implicated in Rochester Bridge's construction: more secure soil would better hold the pilings, and a slower current would lessen the force of water on stone. Humankind's capacity to impose its will on the natural world was therefore ruthlessly tempered by that world. A failure to accommodate environmental imperatives would almost certainly result in the catastrophic collapse of a cultural emblem.

Nature and culture also both impacted the construction itself. Wood, stone, chalk, and iron were molded by engineering principles and art to produce a bridge that stood for half a millennium. The process would have started with the construction of staddles.[34] First, iron-tipped elm piles were driven into the riverbed, establishing a base about 45 feet long by 25 feet wide that was pointed at each end, allowing tides to run in and out with minimal resistance.[35] The tops of these piles were then sawed off at the low-water mark and surrounded by a protective

---

33   William Lambarde, *A Perambulation of Kent* (London: 1576), 303.

34   In the Rochester Bridge accounts, the starling and staddle are referred to as one whole structure, though there is a functional difference between the two. Starlings are constructed to resist the force of a river, and staddles are built to bear the weight of the bridge. I choose to maintain the medieval terminology ("staddle" for the whole structure at the foot of each pier: starling *and* staddle) here.

35   These steps were determined by a firm of contractors who removed the foundations of the medieval bridge after its demolition. See R.H. Britnell, "Rochester Bridge, 1381–1530," in *Traffic and Politics: The Construction and Management of Rochester Bridge, AD 43–1993*, eds. Nigel Yates and James M. Gibson, 43–59 (Woodbridge: Boydell, 1994).

barrier made of additional tied piles, like modern cofferdams. In Rochester, the resulting cavity was packed with chalk — an abundant commodity in Kent that substituted for loose stones and rubble — and finally, the top and sides of each staddle were boarded over with elm planks. In total, twelve of these staddles were built for the Rochester Bridge, resulting in eleven openings, all arched save the seventh opening from the Rochester bank, which was crossed by the royal drawbridge.[36] The roadway and the piers built atop these staddles were then constructed with ragstone, much of it recycled from the previous bridge.

This alone was a feat of civil engineering, but the work was far from over. Maintenance following a "completed" bridge project was constant. As R.H. Britnell notes, "medieval bridges were vulnerable structures, especially when they were large and built over a tidal river, and Rochester Bridge must have been one of the most difficult in England to maintain."[37] In the ten years following the Rochester Bridge's construction, an average of £25 per year was spent on maintenance work, including reinforcing the elm piles, repairing or renewing the wooden framing of the staddles, and packing hundreds of tons of chalk into eroded staddles and the riverbed itself. Careful records report the amount of money spent on bridgework, warden's salaries, administration, upkeep of bridge trust property, rents and taxes, the bridge chapel ("newly erected" in January 1393), and other necessary expenses.[38] All of this suggests a state of perpetual motion, deemed more natural than stasis by fourteenth-century philosopher William of Ockham in his *Opera philosophica*.[39] Beyond being a product of human and hydraulic vectors, and bearing the weight of countless feet in motion (emplaced and between places), the bridge itself transformed in response to the Medway: chalk eroded, ragstone receded, and elm rotted. Most

---

36 Janet Becker, *Rochester Bridge, 1387–1856: A History of its Early Years* (London: Constable & Co., 1930), 9–10.
37 Britnell, "Rochester Bridge, 1381–1530," 47.
38 Becker, *Rochester Bridge*, 13.
39 See Thomas R. Schneider's "Chaucer's Physics: Motion in the *House of Fame*" in the present collection.

man-made structures deteriorate over time, of course, but the micro-movements of bridges are immediately and interminably sensed. Travelers can see foam building around the staddles, hear rushing water, and feel the spray of water on their faces, providing kinesthetic proof that a seemingly static bridge is perhaps better understood to be *kinetic in place*.

The spaces around Rochester Bridge also transformed as a consequence of construction and maintenance. The impact of both on the Kentish landscape was immense, affecting water, wood, and chalk in particular. The effect on the Medway was seen in the forceful current that rushed beneath the ragstone arches, a result of the staddles having substantially decreasing the width of the waterway, which — like at London Bridge — made "shooting the bridge" a favored activity among the daring (some would say reckless) youth. The need for wood, to fabricate piles and the planks that surrounded them, resulted in the deforestation of the downlands' steep, forested slopes. When construction began, Richard II granted bridge contractors carte blanche to take any timber they required from all but the church's land, resulting the felling of thousands of trees in the vicinity of the bridge. In fact, because local reserves were exhausted by the initial construction, wood for replacement piles and planks was shipped from areas as far upriver as Maidstone, with records from the early fifteenth century reporting as many as 200 elms used in a single year.[40]

Chalk, too, was mined at will, with around 100,000 tons of chalk consumed during the first 100 years of bridge maintenance, and as much as 2500 tons of chalk used in a single year.[41] This reallocation of chalk supplies would have affected countless other vocations, including the growth of cherries, an important Kentish export that thrived on chalky soil. So, while the space of a bridge offers an escape from binarism, and therefore meets

---

40 Britnell, "Rochester Bridge, 1381–1530," 63. This statistic reflects the number of elms used in 1444–45; exact information exists only for the years 1436–46.
41 Ibid., 65–66. In 1415 the commonality of the bridge acquired a quarry at Walshes to meet their demand.

the demands of a growing ecocritical field (one that is beginning to look *beyond* nature to the inclusive environments that more accurately represent our hybrid world), we would be remiss to ignore the impact that such a structure has on the ecosystem. It *does* function as one of the few architectural structures that exists coequal with — and not superior to — its immediate environment (i.e., the river), but it *does not* do so without affecting the surrounding, nonhuman ecosystem.

The effects of bridge construction were also felt by the hands, hooves, and bodies that worked the construction site. The manpower demanded by such a difficult project was extraordinary; hundreds of laborers would have to contend with the Medway's current, men and their tools submerged in what must have at times seemed a futile attempt to harness the floods. A fifteenth-century poem appended by Thomas Hearne to his edition of Leland's *Itinerary* narrates this venture for us, with direct reference to the construction of late medieval starling (staddle) bridges in the lowlands. The anonymous poet writes,

> Then the strengthe of the streme astoned hem stronge,
> In labor and lavyng moche money was lore.
> Ther loved hem a ladde was a water man longe,
> He helpe stop the streme til the werke were afore. (39–42)[42]

In this passage, instability reigns: the world is defined by a tumult of water, bodies, and money. Even the efforts of the water man are mitigated. Though he is praised for his work, he can only "helpe" stop the stream, and the poet's use of the ambiguous "afore" reinforces the uncertain nature of the service the "ladde" provides. Is the work behind him, as the preposition "til" implies? Or is it still ahead of him, as the aforementioned records of costly bridge maintenance suggest?[43] The latter is

---

42 *The Itinerary of John Leland the Antiquary,* ed. Thomas Hearne, 9 vols., 2nd ed. (Oxford: 1744–45). Quoted in Harrison, *The Bridges of Medieval England,* 134–35.

43 The MED allows for both readings. See *Middle English Dictionary Online,* s.v. "afore, *adv., prep., conj.,*" http://quod.lib.umich.edu/m/med/.

more likely, given that the poet takes pains to remind his reader, "Thus they were cesed and set all in oon assent / That all the brekynges of the brige the towne bere schulde" (81–2). It is according to Parliamentary procedure, in fact, that the town will be responsible for repairs: "This was preved acte also in the Perlement" (83). Such lines lead a reader to believe that the water man works to "stop the streme" only to have to do so again and again, evoking an infinite regression of pilings, and in so doing reinforcing an understanding of bridges — like their environments and the bodies that bring them into being — as hybrid. Money, labor, raw materials, and rivers circulate in perpetuity, while the bridge itself projects architectural stability.

This poem also advances our thinking about the nature-culture dialectic. The laborers are identified not simply as workingmen, but as "water men." It is as though their skin is permeated by the water in which they are submerged, natural and human fluids comingling to produce a hybrid species that warrants distinction from "land men." One can imagine children on the banks of the Medway marveling at men plunging into the river to tie planks around pilings, breathing as though through gills. A similar appellation occurring regularly in extant records is "tide men," so called because they were paid not by the day, but by the tide. These men worked the gin and the ram to drive piles into the riverbed, work that was restricted to certain states of the tide. Perhaps even more than Hearne's water men, the tide men worked to the rhythms of tidal rivers, their culturally-ingrained patterns of labor forced into alignment with nature's patterns, dictated by the moon rather than the sun.

These processes and the phenomena they engender reveal the degree to which matter and humankind intermingle in the construction of a bridge. The properties and availability of natural resources defined Rochester Bridge's structure, and carefully engineered plans ultimately gave way to natural anomalies. Irregularities in the Medway riverbed, for example, rendered the arches and piers asymmetrical, and the Medway's heavy tides prevented the construction of buildings atop the bridge. Moreover, unlike the spaces surrounding extant transport systems, the fields bordering roads, for example, rivers could not be easily developed. On a bridge, therefore, culture could not fully domesticate and obscure the natural world in/out of which it is built. Yet bridges are always fundamentally cultural, standing *in place* for centuries as testimony to humankind's manipulation of the landscape. Such concessions — humankind to nature and nature to humankind — render Rochester Bridge fundamentally hybrid, built from and embedded in a natural world that reminds passersby of its presence in the sound of water rushing against man-made staddle and cultivated stone.

Bridging Literary Landscapes

As for the place of Rochester Bridge in the Canterbury pilgrimage, we might begin by considering Architect Henry Yevele, who designed Rochester Bridge, the nave of Canterbury Cathedral, *and* the nave of Westminster, while also serving as the warden of London Bridge and caretaker of its chapel. As a consequence of this one man's work, London, Rochester, and Canterbury become an amalgam of architectural continuity: Westminster's nave resembles the arches of Rochester Bridge, which in turn resemble Canterbury Cathedral's nave. Church, state, and civic-mindedness also converge, each manifest in the hybrid structure of the bridge, which mobilized religious, monarchical, and local endeavors alike. These movements were not without regulation, though. As James Smith observes, unregulated movement — characterized by "fluidity" in his work — was a source of anxiety for many medieval writers.[44] Bernard of Cluny, for example, wrote in *De Contemptu Mundi*, "[the world's] position is unfixed, its status is unstable. It goes and it returns, like the sea, now bad and tomorrow even worse."[45] Instability, repre-

---

44 James Smith, "Fluid: A Temporal Ecology," presentation, 47th International Congress on Medieval Studies, Kalamazoo, MI, May 10–13, 2012. See also James Smith, "Fluid," in *Inhuman Nature,* ed. Jeffrey Jerome Cohen, 115–31 (Washington, DC: Oliphaunt Books, 2014).

45 Ronald E. Pepin, trans., *Scorn for the World: Bernard of Cluny's De Contemptu Mundi: The Latin Text with English Translation and an Introduction*

sented here by going and returning, threatened human existence by gesturing toward an apocalyptic chaos, but the mobility played out across Rochester Bridge was not apocalyptic. Instead, mimicking its own simultaneity — representing both nature and culture, movement and stasis — the Rochester Bridge presupposed only *regulated* mobilities, containing what was traditionally understood to be unrestrained kinesis. Indeed, unlike the ferries that could traverse rivers in a multitude of ways, bridges offered mobile bodies only one option.[46] As a consequence, they helped to standardize routes, distilling variable movement toward a given destination into routinized itineraries, and thereby producing a mobile practice best characterized as *structured mobility*: a fettered qualification of a traditionally unfettered term. Such mobilities came to define England and its people, locating medieval identities (like the bridges across which they were played out) in a hybrid category that at once represented humankind's freedom to move, and the strictures placed upon that movement.[47]

In the *Canterbury Tales,* Chaucer depicts one of the most popular structured mobilities of the Middle Ages: pilgrimage. He celebrates the movement of medieval bodies while demonstrating how their perceived "instability" (per Bernard of Cluny) can be regulated by human systems and the built environments in which they take place. In so doing, he finds a middle ground between spatial fixity and the placeless potential of mobility, represented by the *spaces between* the pilgrims' points of departure and destination. First, Chaucer removes London and Canterbury from the *Canterbury Tales*: the pilgrims begin in Southwark, and they never arrive at their destination. This

---

(East Lansing: Colleagues Press, 1991), 1.71.

46 Unless, of course, those bodies were blown off of the bridge and forced to swim to the nearest refuge, an event not unheard of in the Middle Ages. See James M. Gibson, *The Rochester Bridge Trust* (Rochester, Kent: AntidoteFM, 2005)

47 This conceit also evokes Urry's "gamekeeper state," explored by Van Dyke in the present collection, and thereby implicates *animal* movement as well in a discussion of England's mobilities.

suspends the pilgrims in a state of perpetual motion, and erases religio-political centers and landscape features that would unquestionably ground the text. Thomas Becket's tomb, in particular, would have stabilized the pilgrims' journey, its static permanence overshadowing the pilgrims' rich movement. By removing this locus from his frame, Chaucer renders tombs and destinations inconsequential, making the *Canterbury Tales* pilgrimage one that exists almost entirely on the road: an interim space defined by mobility.

He then structures this mobility by locating the pilgrims in Rochester, Sittingbourne, and Harbledown (at 7.1924-6, 3.844-9, and 9.1-4 respectively) — waypoints for travelers in South East England with economies that flourished as a consequence of movement toward Canterbury. Beyond being a religious vocation, pilgrimage was travel, and as such became intertwined with economic systems that anticipated today's tourism industry. Many pilgrims purchased *ampullae* filled with well water from holy places (a practice that linked England's liquid landscape with structured mobilities), and relics/souvenirs multiplied as travelers demanded physical evidence of their successful journeys.[48] Markets grew to accommodate the sale of these souvenirs, and hostels were built to house the weary travelers purchasing them. Pilgrimage thus became a market of sorts, with the loci of circulation and exchange being towns like Rochester: places "by the weye" that grew to accommodate the movement of bodies and material goods. In the frame of the *Canterbury Tales,* it is these places that are prioritized, rendering Southeast England a space defined not by the Tower of London or the Canterbury Cathedral, but by mobile bodies practicing routinized movements in environments defined by (often economically motivated) vectors. Chaucer may not say much about the landscapes through which his pilgrims move, but what he

---

48 See Rosalind and Christopher Brooke, *Popular Religion in the Middle Ages: Western Europe 1000-1300* (London: Thames and Hudson, 1984), and Patrick Geary, *Furta Sacra: The Theft of Relics in the Central Middle Ages* (Princeton: Princeton University Press, 1978).

does say reveals his interest in hybrid categories: meaning is found in a mobile middle.

This macrocosmic structuring of movement in the *Canterbury Tales* — which stipulates that bodies pass through Rochester, Sittingbourne, and Harbledown en route to Canterbury — would then be replicated within each of the three towns Chaucer mentions. Movement through Rochester, for example, would be syphoned across Rochester Bridge: the one available route over the Medway. Given the 1381 collapse of the old medieval bridge, this river crossing could not have been far from Chaucer's mind, especially given his work as Clerk of the King's Works, a job that made him responsible for the construction and maintenance of royal buildings (including bridges). He writes, in the voice of the Host, "'My lord, the Monk […] be myrie of cheere, / For ye shul telle a tale trewely. / Loo Rochestre stant heer faste by!'" (7.1924–6). Here Chaucer offers Rochester as a defining locale in the pilgrims' journey, yet his language unsurprisingly complicates an otherwise straightforward statement, directing our attention beyond the city itself to the more inclusive environment that defines it. Rochester "stands," but more than that, it "stands fast." This suggests stasis, like the (albeit illusory) stasis of the stone bridge that carried pilgrims to Rochester's bank.[49] At the same time, though, "faste" evokes an image of speed, like the rush of the Medway between the bridge's staddles.[50] Chaucer's use of such a multivalent word therefore directs readers to consider both the static city and the movement that defines it, the latter manifest in both the built and liquid landscapes (i.e., the bridge and the river). After drawing his readers' attention to an interim space, he foregrounds the hybridity of this space as both static and mobile, "faste" and "faste."

His embrace of such dynamism extends to the nature-culture dialectic represented by bridges' inclusive environments. We needn't look far to see that Chaucer was intrigued by the world around him. *Parliament of Fowls* describes a meeting between

---

49 *Middle English Dictionary Online,* s.v. "faste, *adv*." def. 2.
50 *Middle English Dictionary Online,* s.v. "faste, *adv*." def. 10.

birds, and the *Nun's Priest's Tale* challenges the boundaries that distinguish animal from human.[51] He also dedicates space to a discussion of deforestation in the *Knight's Tale,* and meditates on the sometimes-unpredictable liquid landscape of the *Franklin's Tale*.[52] These literary moments have been explored in extant scholarship, and there is certainly more to say about how the pilgrims' tales embrace amalgams of nature and culture. A glance at the frame alone, though, reveals Chaucer's attention to the natural environment, perhaps most readily in the familiar opening lines of the *General Prologue*:

> Whan that Aprill with his shoures soote
> The droghte of March hath perced to the roote,
> And bathed every veyne in swich licour
> Of which vertu engendred is the flour;
> Whan Zephirus eek with his sweete breeth
> Inspired hath in every holt and heath
> The tendre croppes, and the yonge soone
> Hath in the Ram his half cours yronne,
> And smale foweles maken melodye,
> That slepen al the nyght with open ye
> (So Priketh hem Nature in hir corages),
> Thanne longen folk to goon on pilgrimages. (1.1–12)

Here both nature and Nature are shown to influence humankind. The wind and rain, personified as Nature in line 11, each inspire "folk" to go on pilgrimage. As Sarah Stanbury writes, "Nature is extrinsic but becomes instrinsic, a force out there in the world as well as within the body; similar to Aristotelian and Platonic concepts of nature, its essence is movement."[53] Like water permeating the skin of water men, Nature permeates ("pricks") humankind's heart, moving us to move. By beginning

---

51 For an ecocritical reading of *Parliament of Fowls,* see Kiser's "Chaucer and the Politics of Nature."
52 On the latter, see Rudd, *Greenery,* 139–48.
53 Stanbury, "Ecochaucer: Green Ethics and Medieval Nature," 11.

the *Tales* with this musing, Chaucer prepares his readers for a hybrid understanding of space that is compounded by the absence of London and Canterbury, and celebrated in the cities he calls to mind. The world represented in the frame of the *Canterbury Tales* is finally both human and nonhuman (with categorical distinctions between the two collapsing from the very start), moving in structured ways to accommodate built environments and natural rhythms alike.

Conclusion: Confluences of Liquid and Literary Landscapes

To close, we might think of the frame as a poetic bridge. It is a space occupied by bodies practicing routinized movement in an environment that is equally natural, "bathed [...] in swich licour / Of which vertu engendred is the flour" (1.3–4), and built, like the "[wyde] chambres and stables" of the Tabard (1.28). But it is also itself hybrid, bridging the poetry of Chaucer's pen (as author), Chaucer's voice (as pilgrim), and the voices of Chaucer's characters. This polyvocality alerts us to how easily categorical distinctions collapse. Yet far from destroying the integrity of Chaucer's project, the collapse of Chaucerian voices produces a harmony that sounds long after a new pilgrim's tale begins. The space of the frame also manifests the building and breaking of metaphorical bridges. Characters erect (albeit often unstable) bridges between disparate genres and themes, and reconcile collapsing collegiality (one may recall the knight who famously instructs the Host to "kisse the Pardoner" [6.965]). In all cases, the interstitial spaces that connect human to inhuman, movement to stasis, and pen to polyphony bear meaning, amplified by the hybrid forms they assume.

Like the bridges it implicitly evokes, then, the frame insists on and celebrates dialectical understanding. The pilgrims themselves are implicated in multiplicities of meaning, and upon reaching Rochester they and the horses on which they ride are both emplaced and between places, producing and presupposing networks of movement and exchange by their being *in transit*. Moreover, they move through and across spaces that cannot be clearly delineated as *either* architectural (cultural) *or* natural; each environment, and especially that of Rochester Bridge, is both. Like the world it represents, then, Chaucer's *Canterbury Tales* is fundamentally hybrid, exemplified by the literal and metaphorical bridges that define it. In the end, these bridges disintegrate categories and enrich our understanding of worlds current and past, lived and literary. We stand to benefit from seeking such bridges in real and imagined landscapes, and embracing the dynamic implications of what lies in the middle.

6

# Chaucer's Physics
## Motion in *The House of Fame*

*Thomas R. Schneider*

Geoffrey Chaucer's *House of Fame* is preoccupied with multiple vectors of chaotic, incessant movement. It is a poem of constant spatial motion, but three moments in particular are strikingly unusual and deserving of unpacking in relation to Chaucer's engagement with the concept of movement. The first is, unsurprisingly, the description of the cage-like wooden structure, sixty miles in diameter, in the valley beyond the House of Fame: perhaps his most potent and strange image of motion. This labyrinthine, multicolored structure is in constant circular motion:

> And ever mo, as swifte as thoughte,
> This queynte hous aboute wente,
> That never mo hyt stille stent.[1]

We know how this House relates to Chaucer's vision for vernacular poetry thanks to dozens of Chaucerians — Steven Kruger, Robert J. Allen, Robert O. Payne, P. M. Kean, Jorg O. Fichte, and others — but in the following pages I am most interested in the link it makes between motion, writing, and thought. Ap-

---

1 Geoffrey Chaucer, *The House of Fame*, in *The Riverside Chaucer*, ed. Larry D. Benson, 347–374, 3rd ed. (Boston: Houghton Mifflin, 1987), 1924–26.

pearing at the climax of the poem, it suggests a broader literary relevance for the work's ceaseless spatial motion.

The second passage is the eagle's speech during the flight through space, a moment unique for its simultaneous enactment of physical motion (what the fourteenth-century English philosopher William of Ockham would call *motu localus* or *motu ad ubi*) and the overt theorization of motion. Even as "Geffrey" is looking beneath him at the "ayerrissh bestes, / Cloudes, mystes, and tempestes, / Snowes, hayles, reynes, wyndes, [...] Alle the wey thurgh which [he] cam" (964–69), the eagle is spouting natural philosophy: specifically, physics. First, he presents a lecture on "kyndely enclyning," a medieval principle similar to the law of gravity:

> Geffrey, thou wost right wel this,
> That every kyndely thing that is
> Hath a kyndely stede ther he
> May best in hyt conserved be;
> Unto which place every thing
> Thorgh his kyndely enclynyng
> Moveth for to come to
> Whan that hyt is awey therfro;
> As thus: loo, thou maist alday se
> That any thing that hevy be,
> As stone, or led, or thyng of wighte,
> And bere hyt never so hye on highte,
> Lat goo thyn hand, hit falleth doun.
> Ryght so seye I be fyr or soun,
> Or smoke or othe thynges lyghte;
> Alwey they seke upward on highte. (729–44)

And the eagle continues speaking, further proposing, specifically citing Plato and Aristotle, that "speech is soun" [speech is sound], that "soun is noghte but eyr ybroken" [sound is broken air], that it therefore desires to travel upward in rings through the air like a pond into which a stone has been thrown, and that it is therefore possible for all sounds in the world to eventually reach a single place: the chaotic nest that gathers all news.[2] The key to this theory is that sound "moveth first an ayr aboute, / And of this movynge, oute of doute, / Another eyr anoon ys meved" (811–13). This lengthy philosophizing tends to seem odd to us in such a kinetic context. The words themselves mirror Ockham's words about projectile motion in the *Expositio in libros physicorum aristotelis*: "and therefore one part moved with a natural motion pushes the other, and if the other succeeds, because of that the other moves violently, which moved it moves the other either to its proper place more quickly than it is moved by itself, to another place."[3] The natural inclining of light and heavy things, or *levia* and *gravia*, is also a recurring topic in Ockham's writings. This section of poetry argues, in a scientifically informed way, that speech, including the reading of *The House of Fame* itself, is motion.

The third moment in the poem is from still earlier, when the eagle comes hurtling out of the sky and tears Geffrey out of his wandering on the plain:

This egle, of which I have yow told,
That shon with fethres as of gold,
Which that so hye gan to sore,
I gan beholde more and more
To se the beaute and the wonder;
But never was ther dynt of thonder,
Ne that thing that men calle fouder,
That smot sometyme a tour to powder
And in his swifte comynge brende,
That so swithe gan descende

---

[2] Ibid., 762, 765, 785–821.
[3] "Et ideo una pars mota motu naturali aliam impellit, et si succedit alia, propter quod alia violenter movetur, quae mota movet aliam vel ad locum proprium velocius quam moveretur ex se, vel ad alium locum [...]" (William of Ockham, *Opera philosophica*, vol. V: *Expositio in libros physicorum aristotelis* [St. Bonaventure: Editiones Instituti Franciscani Universitatis S Bonaventurae, 1974], 626).

As this foule, when hyt beheld
That I a-roume was in the field. (529-40)

These lines together communicate a multi-layered flash of speed, violence, beauty, and wonder. The eagle's descent is overlaid with images of a flame, a percussion of thunder, and a lightning bolt reducing a stone tower to dust. In sharp contrast to the stillness emphasized by the "ymages" and "portreytures" of the Temple of Glass, words of movement and speed dominate these lines: "sore," "smot," "swifte," "comynge," "swithe," "descend," "a-roume." In these three passages, we see a picture of movement that is insistently present, aesthetically powerful, and above all a complex blend of order and chaos — exemplified by "kyndely enclyning" and the Whirling Wicker.

Because of the nature of this representation of movement, I contend that we should pay attention to Ockham's physics as it relates to motion in this poem, especially sections of his *Brevis summa libri physicorum* and his *Expositio in libros physicorum aristotelis* (both written in the early 1320s)— in part because there is reason to believe that Chaucer may have.

## Ockham's Physics

Chaucer's understanding of motion was inflected by his knowledge of the philosophical and scientific discourses of his time. The extent to which he was a "scholar" has long been the subject of debate, but there is widespread consensus that he was a well-read and educated writer.[4] We know from Chaucer's allu-

---

4 Kathryn Lynch provides an excellent summary of this debate, beginning with Caxton and other early writers who imagined Chaucer as a philosopher, including the poet's first (inaccurate) biographer John Leland, who described him as a profound scholar in the fields of logic, oratory, poetry, philosophy, and mathematics. Derek Pearsall proposes that Chaucer "was widely read, and used his reading intelligently, but he was not a scholar," and Kathryn Lynch welcomes this caution but emphasizes Chaucer's scholarly expertise. Kathryn L. Lynch, *Chaucer's Philosophical Visions* (Woodbridge: D.S. Brewer, 2000), 16-17. Derek Pearsall, *The Life of Geoffrey Chaucer: A Critical Biography* (Oxford: Blackwell, 1992), 32.

sions that he was familiar with some Scholastic philosophy and, importantly for this study, physics. In the fourteenth century, physics — including prominently the physics of motion — was studied within the category of natural philosophy, and such studies were predominantly commentaries on Aristotle. In this context, the importance of the thought and writing of William of Ockham is almost undisputed.[5] As Paul Vincent Spade observes, "standard histories have long recognized that the three most important figures in the philosophy of the High Middle Ages were Thomas Aquinas (1224/5–74), John Duns Scotus (c. 1266–1308), and William of Ockham (c. 1288–1347).[6] Ockham's school of thought, nominalism, is understood as having been dominant, or at least "widely discussed," for around fifty years in the mid- to late-fourteenth century in the intellectual centers of Oxford, Avignon, Paris, and Munich.[7] These centers controlled the philosophical climate of much of Western Europe, and Ockham, an Englishman, was particularly influential in England, where he experienced his most prolific period of writing (1321–1324) including his works of physics.[8] Although he is often known for his theology and later political writings (while in Avignon and Munich), this subject was of significant interest to him, his ideas were well known to the educated readership in late fourteenth-century England, and, in comparison to Scotus or Aquinas, his contributions to physics were particularly groundbreaking.

---

5  William J. Courtenay has claimed that "Ockham is better seen not as the leader or center of movement but as one of many contemporary authors whose opinions were widely discussed, sometimes accepted, and sometimes rejected" (William J. Courtenay, "The Academic and Intellectual Worlds of Ockham," in *The Cambridge Companion to Ockham*, ed. Paul Vincent Spade, [Cambridge: Cambridge University Press, 1999], 28). Despite this appropriate caution, Courtenay still treats Ockham's writings as important and "widely discussed," and most scholars still see Ockham as more of a central figure than his contemporaries.

6  Ibid., 1.

7  Ibid., 27.

8  Ibid., 23.

Aristotle's physics were the standard at the time, and Ockham supports some of these theories while radically revising others. One element that he maintains is the critical importance of motion to the understanding of existence. He engages with and confirms one of Aristotle's prominent conclusions: "for if we are ignorant of what a motion is, we are of necessity ignorant of what nature is."[9] The subjects of projectile motion (the motion of a thrown object, for example), planetary/heavenly movement, and self-propelled/willed motion dominate his physics, falling under the category *motu localis* or *motu ad ubi* ("local motion," or movement through space). He begins to depart from Aristotle, however, in the details that control and describe these motions. Three related and unique aspects of his physics of motion are of particular relevance to Chaucer's poetry: his description of space, his argument about the complex forces that cause movement, and his explanation of continued, potentially perpetual, *yet irregular* motion.

First, like Henri Lefebvre and other postmodern theorists who characterize space as substantive and produced by movements, like the post-Einsteinian physics of space-time, Ockham rejects the idea that space is a void.[10] For Ockham, however, it is not real as a substance, either. The concept of place (*locus*) appears frequently in his writing, but almost always subordinated to motion. The primary function of *locus* as a concept is to differentiate movements. If place exists — for Ockham, it is a conceptual framework but not a substance — it is because it is possible to move from place to place.[11] The primary definition of local motion found in Ockham's writings — representa-

---

9 William of Ockham, *Opera philosophica*, vol. VI: *Brevis summa libri physicorum, Summula philosophiae naturalis, et Quaestiones in libros physicorum aristotelis* (St. Bonaventure: Editiones Instituti Franciscani Universitatis S. Bonaventurae, 1974), 39; William of Ockham, *Ockham on Aristotle's Physics: A Translation of Ockham's Brevis summa libri physicorum,* trans. Julian A. Davies (St. Bonaventure: The Franciscan Institute, St. Bonaventure University, 1989), 39.
10 André Goddu, *The Physics of William of Ockham* (Leiden: Brill, 1984), 203.
11 William of Ockham, *Ockham on Aristotle's Physics,* 55; Goddu, *The Physics of William of Ockham,* 215–16.

tive of his nominalism — is the condition in which an object exists partially in one place and partially in another.[12] Ockham determines that to understand the cosmos, we should look to motion rather than space or place, although place is a critical concept. Place, such as it appears in Ockham, is not only colored or characterized by motion, but its very existence as a concept is *only* necessitated because of the existence of motion. The intertwining of space and motion is further emphasized as Ockham discusses the shape of space; specifically, he mentions that motion through a winding space (*spatium tortuosam*) is irregular.[13] In regard to this concept of (ir)regularity, he claims that "*motus regularis est magis unus quam motus irregularis*" [a regular motion is more one than an irregular motion], but also, notably, that "*regularitas et irregularitas* […] *convenient omni specie motus*" [regularity and irregularity belong to every species of motion.][14] This is one of many hints at motion as plural in Ockham, in contrast to the unity and relative simplicity of the Aristotelian system: Ockham resists defining motion in a single category or as produced by a single cause.

Second, in relation to one ancient question — why does an object continue to move after it has left the hand that threw it? — Ockham introduced more complex forces than had been previously considered. A number of explanations for continued projectile motion were in circulation at the time, including the idea, supported by Aristotle and Averroës, that the "throwing hand" moves air, and that this air moves the projectile. Ockham's response is not to directly refute this theory, but to complicate it, demonstrating that "violent" and "natural" motions, as well as intrinsic and extrinsic forces, are all involved. The following is a longer selection from the passage in his *Expositio in libros physicorum aristotelis,* mirrored strikingly by Chaucer's eagle:

---

12   Ockham, *Opera philosophica,* vol. V: *Expositio in libros physicorum aristotelis,* 507–22.
13   Ibid., V:409.
14   Ibid., V:411.

To this it can be said that air moves the projected not as if one moving uniformly with one motion, but because air is easily divisible, air is divided in many parts, one of which is moved more quickly than another actual cause. And therefore one part moved with a natural motion pushes the other, and if the other succeeds, because of that the other is moved violently, which moved it moves the other either to its proper place more quickly than it is moved by itself, or to another place. And so diverse parts of diverse moved things by themselves move the projected. And then when it is asked of that moving whether it is moved from itself or from another, I say that something moving is moved from itself and something from the other, and therefore the state obtains not with respect to many things moved from themselves. And therefore, although the projected is moved by an extrinsic thing and violently, nevertheless there are diverse moving things there, which are moved of themselves and not by something extrinsic.[15]

No one force is responsible for the continued motion of the projectile: its motion seems to be caused by its natural tendency to move to its proper place (for a heavy object, downward), the diverse and irregular divisions that appear in the air, the initial hand that threw the object, and a mysterious internal impulse to continue moving. This last force is particularly noteworthy:

---

15 "Ad hoc dici potest quod aer movet proiectum non quasi unum movens uniforme uno motu, sed quia aer est faciliter divisibilis, aer in multas partes dividitur, quarum una velocius movetur quam alia ex alia cause actuali. Et ideo una pars mota motu naturali aliam impellit, et si succedit alia, propter quod alia violenter movetur, quae mota movet aliam vel ad locum proprium velocius quam moveretur ex se, vel ad alium locum, et sic diversae partes diversae motae a seipsis movent proiectum, et tunc quando quaereritur illud movens, aut movetur ex se aut ex alio, dico quod aliquod movens movetur ex se et aliquid ex altero, et ideo est status non ad primum proiiciens sed ad aliam partem aeris pulsem a proiiciente, et postea ex se motam vel forte perveniendum est ad talia multa mota ex se, et ideo quamvis proiectum moveatur ab extrinseco et violenter, tamen diversa sunt ibi moventia quae ex se moventur et non ab extrinseco" (ibid., V:626).

as he writes elsewhere, "*corpora simplicia et universaliter omnia gravia et levia possunt moveri ex se quia principium effectivum motus eorum est aliquid in eis subiective existens*" [simple bodies, and all heavy and light bodies, can move on their own because they have that which is the principle or source of their motion within themselves][16] This impulse, combined with the various forces of projector and the diverse separations in the air (emphatically *not* uniform, regular, or singular) comprise a medieval theory of motion that was unparalleled at the time for its nuance and complexity.

Finally, and relatedly, part of Ockham's contribution to the understanding of motion is his apparent preoccupation with its persistence. Motion, in Ockham's estimation, is a more fundamental state to existence than rest — a fact that he emphasizes more than his predecessors. For example, although he concludes, as mentioned above, that all objects contain the principle of motion in themselves, they do not contain the principle of rest: the ability to stop on their own.[17] Although he concedes that "*animal potest moveri per aliquod spatium est potest etiam quiescere*" [an animate thing can move through a space and can also stop],[18] moving remains, in his analysis, more natural and less "violent" than stopping. This internally-generated motion is critical to his critique of Aristotle's principle, expressed by Ockham as "*in omnia tali motu movens propinquum et motum sunt simul*" [in every such thing moved, the nearest moving and moved are together], meaning that, when an object is projected it needs the movement of the projector to be transferred onto it in some way to continue moving. Instead, Ockham argued that an object in motion can continue to move *of itself,* without an external mover, because all things contain this potential motion and tend toward motion.[19] In fact, departing from Aristotle, Ockham determined that continued, perpetual motion requires

---

16  Ibid., V:371.
17  Ibid., V:186, 371.
18  Ibid.
19  Goddu, *The Physics of William of Ockham,* 203.

no explanation or cause.[20] The only explanation truly needed for motion is the distance from one place to another; for Ockham, if there is distance, it is natural for an object to cross that distance.

In summary, Ockham refuted and built on Aristotelian physics by claiming that: (1) the concept of space/place is necessitated and shaped by motion; (2) motion is a network of more complex and diverse forces than had been previously believed; and (3) motion is an impulse internal to all (even inanimate) things, potentially infinite and continuous, and the tendency to cross an intervening space is more natural than to remain in stasis.

## Motion in Chaucer's Poem

When we turn back to the moments in *The House of Fame* mentioned above, we see these principles embodied in poetry. This embodiment can be understood to begin even before the eagle's decent, however, in the dreamer's rejection of the Temple of Venus. As soon as Geffrey — said to be as exhausted as one who had just taken a pilgrimage — falls asleep, we as readers arrive at this temple, "ymad of glass" (120).[21] Once inside, the narrative slows to a crawl, losing action in favor of description. The dreamer lists what he sees there in a tone of wonder: "moo ymages / Of gold, stondynge in sondry stages, / And moo ryche tabernacles, / And with perre moo pynacles, / And moo curiouse portrytures, / And queynte maner of figures / Of olde werk, than I saugh ever" (121–27). The repetition of words for "pictures": "ymages," "portrytures," and "figures," emphasize the stillness of the place. Rather than a living Venus, as we see in *The Parliament of the Fowls,* this place is only identified as her temple by her "portreyture" on a wall (131). Not only are these images static, they are specifically referred to as "olde werk," building on the developing image of a resplendent, yet abandoned, museum. The dreamer's response to this place, considering what

---

20 Ibid., 228.
21 "And file on slepe wonder sone, / As he that wery was forgo / On pilgrimage myles two / To the corseynt Leonard." Chaucer, *The House of Fame,* 116–17.

we know of him from the poem's opening, makes perfect sense: he reads, at great length. A striking portion of the poem (some 316 lines) are devoted to the story of Dido and Aeneas, a part of which is present in still images on the walls of the temple. This story is the slowest moment in a rapidly-paced poem; narrative action is replaced here with hundreds of lines of reflection and digression while the dreamer lingers.

Line 476, "but now wol I goo out and see," marks the turn of this dream vision; from this point forward, Chaucer's narrative will stand in sharp contrast to what we see in Venus' Temple of Glass: motion replaces stillness, newness replaces "old werke," and fierce, sharp moments of beauty replace lingering meditation. The narrator's progress here, as Chaucer turns away from old stories, is reminiscent of Ockham's complication and revitalization of the Aristotelian theoretical system of motion. The dreamer's exit "at the wiket" breathes life into the poem and, at this point, a powerful embodiment of the connection between motion and aesthetics explodes into the vision as Jove's eagle screams toward Geffrey where he wanders in the empty plain surrounding the temple.

The trajectory of *The House of Fame* brings the dreamer, carried by his eagle guide, to the labyrinthine structure that gives the poem its name "right even in myddes of the weye / Betwixen hevene and erthe and see" (714–15), a crossroads in space, where the conflation of language and movement, already theorized, is depicted as a physical place. This third and final book of the poem, introduced through an invocation to Apollo, "god of science and lyght" (1091), is characterized by truly chaotic movement. The eagle having departed, the dreamer is forced to climb "with alle payne" (1118) up a sheer cliff-face of ice. Images of thunder and tempest return to Chaucer's poetic line as Geffrey approaches what are revealed to be two buildings: the sound he hears is "lyk betynge of the see […] ayen the roches holowe, / Whan tempest doth the shippes swalowe" (1034–36) or "lyk the last humblynge / After the clappe of a thundringe" (1039–40). The climactic spectacle is characterized by deafening noise, which, as this poem has taken great pains to inform us, is to be understood as spatial motion — physical movement, even breaking, of the air. The scene inside the House of Fame is everything that the Temple of Glass was not: swarms of people coming and going, every kind of entertainer imaginable in late medieval English society performing, the great horn blowing either good or bad fame across the face of the earth. But the most stunning image of motion in this poem is the source of the noise originally heard: the House positioned in a valley under the castle, "that Domus Dedaly, / That Laboryntus cleped ys, / Nas mad so wonderlych, ywis, / Ne half so queyntelych ywrought" (1920–23).

The multiple layers of images of movement embodied in this place unroll as it is described. The first worth noting is the initial comparison used to describe it: it is like the Labyrinth, or "Domus Dedaly." The labyrinth, as a structure, is built for movement alone; its twists, turns, corners, and dead ends exist to facilitate unpredictable, wandering, and confused movement. It is the physical embodiment, or a kind of physical mapping or writing on the land "in a scrawling hand," as theorist Henri Lefebvre might note, of a kind of intensely irregular motion.[22] Donald Howard, in relation to this image in Chaucer's poem, reminds us that the *domus Dedali* was a kind of design painted on or carved into medieval church walls and floors in the shape of a labyrinth, used for penance. Those seeking to do penance for their sins would either trace the path of their movement through the labyrinth with their fingers or crawl upon the image on the floor as a substitute for pilgrimage.[23] The *domus Dedali,* then, can be

---

[22] "Traversed now by pathways and patterned by networks, natural space changes: one might say that practical activity writes upon nature, albeit in a scrawling hand, and that this writing implies a particular representation of space. Places are marked, noted, named. [...] Paths are more important than the traffic they bear, because they are what endures in the form of the reticular patterns [...]. Could it be called a text, or a message?" (Henri Lefebvre, *The Production of Space,* trans. Donald Nicholson-Smith [Malden: Blackwell, 1991], 117).

[23] Donald R. Howard, "Flying through Space: Chaucer and Milton," in *Milton and the Line of Vision,* ed. Joseph Anthony Wittreich, Jr., (Madison: University of Wisconsin Press, 1975), 13–14.

understood as a static image that also embodies and facilitates movement, literally and insofar as it figures travel abroad.

The motion of this place, as mentioned above, is also far more obviously literal than the roaring of its noise and its association with the labyrinth. This massive building, referred to as "the Whirling Whicker" by Pierro Boitani, perpetually spins in place.[24] The description of this place embodies pluralism and complex motion. In terms of its construction, while the walls in the Temple of Glass were starkly polished and ordered, this "house" is like an enormous nest — an image of seemingly disordered construction through a natural, earthy, and random process. To augment this image of plurality, the twigs of which it is built are wildly multicolored — "and al thys hous of which y rede, / Was mad of twigges, falwe, rede, / And grene eke, and somme weren white" (1935–37). Doorways are controllers of movement through an architectural space — as Chaucer, living over one of the "principle" gates of London, would have been more aware than most — and this place seems to be constructed more of doorways and holes than of walls.[25] This multitude of doors defines it as a space of multi-directional and chaotic movement, in opposition to the one or two doors of the Temple of Glass, even without the constant spinning motion of the entire structure. Finally, the crowd of people inside are also those characterized by their travel over land and sea: "shipmen and pilgrims" (2122).

Generations of Chaucer scholars have recognized the links between this house of twigs and Chaucer's ideas about poetry, especially in relation to issues of poetic authority, form, the vernacular, and the eventual creation of the *Canterbury Tales*.[26] This

---

24 Piero Boitani, "Chaucer's Labyrinth: Fourteenth-Century Literature and Language," *The Chaucer Review* 17, no. 3 (1983): 197–220.
25 Chaucer, *The House of Fame,* 1945–46.
26 Steven Kruger, one of many such examples, writes: "As has been widely recognized, the House of Fame forcefully and explicitly calls attention to its own poetic status," and that "it also examines the processes of transmission and transformation by which authoritative traditions may be questioned and finished poems themselves unmade and reinvented." Steven F. Kruger,

place embodies, in dramatic contrast to the Temple of Glass and its static images of classical stories, a shift from the authority of classical sources to that of the words of the present moment, and words spoken by *all* people, a profoundly important move in relation to his later poetry and the development of English vernacular literature. Most importantly for this study, however, the words of all people, as the eagle has told us, are formed of physically moving air rippling toward this place, arriving in spoken fragments as a cacophony of sound. This motion is wildly complicated, eternal, physical, and consistently favored in the narrative over stasis and order. The connections between this poetic expression of motion and Ockham's revisions of Aristotelian physics are striking.

**Closing Thoughts**

In recent scholarship, Chaucer has been linked to Ockham and Ockhamism, and the poet's knowledge of at least some of the philosopher's works and ideas has been established. Helen Ruth Andretta has related *Troilus and Criseyde* to Ockhamism, and,

---

"Imagination and the Complex Movement of Chaucer's *House of Fame*," *The Chaucer Review* 28, no. 2 (1993): 117–34, at 118. Other studies that call attention to *The House of Fame*, not only as a poem about poetry but about authority and poetic transmission include: Robert J. Allen, "A Recurring Motif in Chaucer's 'House of Fame,'" *The Journal of English and Germanic Philology* 55, no. 3 (1956): ; Robert O. Payne, *The Key of Remembrance, a Study of Chaucer's Poetics* (New Haven: Yale University Press, 1963); J.A.W. Bennett, *Chaucer's 'Book of Fame': An Exposition of 'the House of Fame,'* (Oxford: Clarendon Press, 1968); P.M. Kean, *Chaucer and the Making of English Poetry* (London: Routledge and K. Paul, 1972); Jorg O. Fichte, *Chaucer's 'Art Poetical': A Study in Chaucerian Poetics* (Tübingen: Narr Tübingen, 1980); Karla Taylor, *Chaucer Reads "The Divine Comedy"* (Stanford: Stanford University Press, 1989); Martin Irvine, "Medieval Grammatical Theory and Chaucer's *House of Fame*," *Speculum* 60 (1985): 850–76; Delany, *Chaucer's House of Fame: The Poetics of Skeptical Fideism* (Gainesville: The University Press of Florida, 1994); Jacqueline T. Miller, "The Writing on the Wall: Authority and Authorship in Chaucer's *House of Fame*," *The Chaucer Review* 17, no.2 (1982): 95–115; Katherine Zieman, "Chaucer's Voys," *Representations* 60 (1997): 70–91. William S. Wilson, "Scholastic Logic in Chaucer's House of Fame," *The Chaucer Review* 1, no. 3 (1967): 181–84.

although Kathryn L. Lynch focuses on specific philosophical doctrines and denies Chaucer's affiliation with any single philosopher, she argues extensively for seeing Chaucer as a kind of nominalist, (the school in which Ockham was the primary figure and innovator) and influenced by several of Ockham's, as well as other contemporary philosophers', ideas.[27] A.J. Minnis, in his representation of Chaucer's philosophical climate, gives Ockham a prominent place.[28] The relationship between Ockham's *physics* and Chaucer's poetry, however, has received little attention. The dominance of Ockham's thinking in England while Chaucer was writing in 1374 and Chaucer's surprisingly complex interaction with Aristotelian/Ockhamist concepts of motion make it likely that the poet was at least aware of these ideas in circulation, and we know that he was working directly with the Aristotelian texts with which Ockham was also engaging—quite probably via Ockham's commentaries, considering manuscript circulation. It is likely that Chaucer was influenced by Ockham's physics when he wrote *The House of Fame,* but at very least he was doing something analogous in poetry to what Ockham was doing in physics. Chaucer's poem is preoccupied with motion as a fundamental state, and he is a "complicator" of ideas about motion. His dream vision is truly one in which, in Ockham's words, "*diversa sunt ibi moventia*" [diverse moving things are there].[29] From his position surrounded by movement in his rooms above Aldgate, Chaucer created a kinetic vision of plurality and resistance to stasis. Although the road to Canterbury may continue to be Chaucer's most famous image of movement, the flash of the eagle's appearance and what follows reveal, in this early work, Chaucer's philosophically nuanced creation of motion through poetry.

---

27 Lynch, *Chaucer's Philosophical Visions,* 15. Helen Ruth Andretta, *Chaucer's Troilus and Creseyde: A Poet's Response to Ockhamism* (New York: Peter Lang, 1997).
28 A. J. Minnis, *Chaucer and Pagan Antiquity* (Cambridge: D.S. Brewer, 1982).
29 Ockham, *Opera philosophica,* vol.V: *Expositio in libros physicorum aristotelis,* 626.

# Contributors

**James L. Smith** is Visiting Research Fellow at the Trinity Long Room Hub Arts and Humanities Research Institute, Trinity College Dublin. He focuses on intellectual history, medieval abstractions and visualization schemata, environmental humanities, and water history. His first monograph is entitled *Water in Medieval Intellectual Culture: Case-Studies from Twelfth-Century Monasticism* (Brepols, 2017). James is the co-editor of a themed collection of the Open Library of the Humanities on "New Approaches to Medieval Water Studies," forthcoming in 2018. He is currently shaping a digital/environmental humanities project entitled "Deep Mapping Spiritual Interactions with Ireland's Lakes: The Case of Lough Derg." James blogs at https://scrivenersmith.com/.

**Christopher Roman** is Professor of English at Kent State University. His various publications, lectures, and presentations investigate the entangled themes of queer theory and queer theology in medieval vernacular religion, gender and sexuality in the life of anchorites and hermits, animal studies and ecology in medieval literature, and the emergent field of sound studies and the sound of the Middle Ages. His first book, *Domestic Mysticism in Julian of Norwich and Margery Kempe* (2005) interrogates queer family formation in medieval mystical texts. His new book, *Queering Richard Rolle* (2017), investigates the queer identity of the medieval hermit, Richard Rolle. His new work investigates the use of sound in the medieval Biblical exegesis of the High Middle Ages and in the work of Chaucer. He is currently working on a new edition of Richard Rolle's Middle English works to be published by the Medieval English Text Series. He serves as the Associate Editor of *The Chaucer Review*.

**Jennie Friedrich** received her Ph.D. in English from the University of California at Riverside, specializing in medieval literature. Friedrich's research focuses primarily on cultural approaches to travel and bodily injury in medieval literature, and her most recent work employs theories on disability to question normative notions of the body and its relation to movement in medieval narratives of travel. Upon graduation in spring 2015, she was hired as a full-time lecturer in the University Writing Program, where she integrates medieval texts into her curriculum as she continues her own research: a book-length study of travel-related damage that examines literary tropes of injury and traveling body parts as physical processes rather than metaphors that transcend the materiality of the body.

**Robert Stanton** is Associate Professor of English at Boston College, specializing in Old and Middle English Language and Literature, translation studies, and critical animal studies. He is the author of *The Culture of Translation in Anglo-Saxon England* (Boydell & Brewer, 2002) as well as numerous articles on saints' lives, mystics, and medieval animals. He is currently working on a book entitled *Holy Signs and Fruitful Toil: Animal Voice and Signification in Anglo-Saxon England*.

**Carolynn Van Dyke**, Francis A. March Professor Emerita of English at Lafayette College, is the author of *The Fiction of Truth: Structures of Meaning in Narrative and Dramatic Allegory* (Cornell, 1985) and *Chaucer's Agents: Cause and Representation in Chaucerian Narrative* (Fairleigh Dickinson, 2005). She is editor of *Rethinking Chaucerian Beasts* (Palgrave, 2012); her essays in medieval animal studies have appeared in *Studies in the Age of Chaucer* and *postmedieval*.

**Sarah Breckenridge Wright** is an Assistant Professor in Duquesne University's Department of English, where she specializes in medieval literature. Her articles on movement, geography, and memory in medieval literature include "The Soil's Holy Bodies: The Art of Chorography in William of Malmesbury's Gesta Pontigicum Anglorum," *Studies in Philology* 111, no. 4 (2014), and "Cognitive Discoveries and Constructed Mindscapes: Reading the Grail Castle as a Mnemonic Device," *Modern Language Review* 106, no. 4 (2011).

**Thomas R. Schneider** is an Assistant Professor of English at California Baptist University, where he teaches a wide range of literature and language courses with an emphasis on medieval literature. He earned his Ph.D. in English from the University of California, Riverside, in 2013. His ongoing research and writing is about early British literature with a special interest in movement—from ideas about the nature of the quest to the way these stories create a sense of motion and rhythm for the reader. He lives in Riverside, California.

www.ingramcontent.com/pod-product-compliance
Lightning Source LLC
Chambersburg PA
CBHW051131160426
43195CB00014B/2433